TRUE CRIME CASE HISTORIES

Volume 7

JASON NEAL

iDigital Group

Cover photos of:

Stephen McDaniel (top-left)

Omaima Nelson (top-right)

Gerard John Schaefer (bottom-left)

Sky McDonough (bottom-right)

Also by Jason Neal

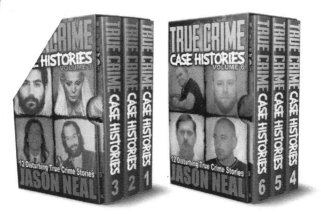

Looking for more?? I am constantly adding new volumes of True Crime Case Histories and all books are also available in paperback, hardcover and audiobooks.

Check out the complete series on Amazon:

Amazon US / Amazon UK

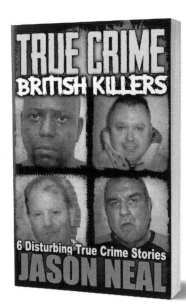

**FREE Bonus Book
For My Readers**

**Click to get
your free copy!**

As my way of saying "Thank you" for downloading, I'm giving away a FREE true crime book I think you'll enjoy.

http://truecrimecasehistories.com

Just click the link above to let me know where to send your free gift!

Choose Your Free True Crime Audiobook

Add Audible Narration and Keep the Story Going! Plus Get a FREE True Crime Audiobook!

Switch between listening to an audiobook and reading on your Kindle. **Plus choose your first audiobook for FREE!** Audible US / Audible UK

CONTENTS

INTRODUCTION

If you're familiar with the previous books in the True Crime Case Histories series, you already know that I start each book with a brief warning. Real true crime is not for everyone. The stories in this book represent humanity at its absolute worst. Pure evil. Television crime shows and news articles often skip the gruesome parts of true crime stories. The real details are just too grisly for the average viewer or reader.

In my books, however, I do my best to include the details, regardless of how unsettling they may be. Each story requires hours of research. I search through old newspaper articles, court documents, police reports, autopsy results, and first-hand descriptions. Some of the specifics can be disconcerting. I choose to include the details not to shock, but to give the reader a deeper view into the mind of the killer. Although it's unlikely any of us will understand the motives of a diabolical monster, the level of depravity will keep you turning pages.

That being said, if you are overly squeamish about the details of true crime, this book may not be for you. If you're okay with it... then let's begin.

———

Volume Seven of True Crime Case Histories highlights twelve new stories taking place over the past fifty years. You'll read about a law enforcement officer that took advantage of the trust associated with his uniform. His brutal reign of terror lasted eight years. It took the bravery of two young women that escaped his grasp to bring him down.

There's the story of the recent law school graduate with a crush on his neighbor. Rather than asking her out on a date, he stalked and spied on his classmate, eventually taking her life. There's also the heartbreaking story of a single mom, drowning in debt, that did the unthinkable for insurance money.

Seven of the stories in this book feature women killers, two of which took the time to meticulously dismember their victims—a task that can take great strength. Another woman manipulated her two teenage boys into killing for her. Yet another woman staged an elaborate hoax to get rid of her loving husband rather than go through the agony of a messy divorce.

You'll also read of a sadistic group of up to twelve killers that took joy in abducting and torturing young men in Australia. Sadly, only one of the mysterious group has been brought to justice.

These and other stories in this book are revolting and disconcerting, but they're true. These things really happen in the world. Although we will never fully understand the criminal mind, at least we can be better informed.

I am constantly looking for new stories for future books and I prefer stories that can't already be found all over the Internet. I look for stories that have gone largely unreported other than the original articles in local newspapers. Two of the stories in this book were submitted to me by readers. To those of you who have sent me story ideas—a big thank you! I'm always looking for more. If you remember an interesting story that happened years ago, has been forgotten, and you'd like to see it written about, please send me any details you can remember and I will do my best to research them.

Lastly, I encourage you to join my mailing list for discounts, updates, and a free book. You can sign up for that here:

http://TrueCrimeCaseHistories.com

THE GEORGIA VOYEUR

Twenty-seven-year-old Lauren Giddings had been the first of her family to attend college. Her relatives back in Maryland were proud that she would soon have a career as a public defender. Lauren had just graduated from Mercer University's Walter F. George School of Law in Macon, Georgia.

Although she had finished school, the tall, beautiful, green-eyed blonde spent the final week of June 2011 studying for her upcoming bar exam. Lauren's sister knew she would be spending long hours preparing for the exam, so it didn't raise any concerns when Lauren hadn't returned her text messages.

Lauren had lived in Barrister Hall Apartments, directly across the street from her law school, for the past three years. Although she loved her apartment's location, she had mentioned to her sisters and classmates that she frequently had an eerie feeling someone had been inside her apartment while she was away. She had noticed things in her apartment appeared to be arranged differently than the way she had left them. At least she thought so... but she couldn't be sure.

Lauren Giddings

Throughout the past year, Lauren had considered moving to a different apartment complex, but the location was so close to school that it was hard to give up that convenience. Plus, now that she had just graduated, she planned to move to Atlanta the following Thursday, anyway.

———

On a Saturday afternoon, Lauren visited with her friends during the day and went home in the evening. Late that night, Lauren emailed a close friend saying that she was afraid to stay in her apartment alone that night. Something just didn't feel right. That was the last communication anyone had with Lauren.

During the following week, Lauren's friends couldn't reach her. They called her cell phone and knocked on her door, but there was no response. Her friends called the police when they hadn't heard from her for several days.

Police met one of Lauren's classmates at her apartment for a welfare check and knocked on the door. Peeking through the window, they couldn't see much. There was no sign that someone had broken in and nothing seemed out of the ordinary from the outside. The officers spoke briefly to a few neighbors in the area, but concluded that she just wasn't home. The police told her friend not to worry. Lauren's boyfriend, an Atlanta lawyer, was in California at the time and the officers suggested she may have taken a flight to spend time with him.

Lauren's classmate was not convinced. She was a very responsible and professional young woman; it wasn't like Lauren to just disappear. Plus, she would never have gone on a trip just days before her bar exam. The classmate called Lauren's sister Kaitlyn in Maryland, who confirmed that she had not heard from Lauren either.

Kaitlyn, however, knew that Lauren hid a key under a potted plant on her balcony and gave permission for the girl to enter her apartment. Several of Lauren's friends arrived at the upstairs apartment to get the key and check inside. Stephen McDaniel, who had lived in the apartment next to Lauren for the past three years, joined the search. Twenty-five-year-old McDaniel was a classmate of Lauren's that had also just graduated and was preparing for the bar exam.

When the group entered Lauren's apartment late Wednesday night, the first thing they noticed was a door-jammer security bar lying next to the door. Normally, she would have propped the security bar against the door under the handle and wedged it against the floor to prevent an intruder from entering. Other than that, there was no sign anyone had forcefully entered the apartment and there was no sign of Lauren. Strangely, her belongings were still there. Her cell phone, wallet, driver's license, passport, and car keys. Her car was still parked in the parking lot. She definitely hadn't gone on a trip without bringing her identification. Lauren's friends again called Macon police and filed a missing person report just before 2:00 A.M.

Police arrived early on Thursday morning to search the apartment and neighborhood, as well as interview neighbors and classmates. Television news crews were quickly on the scene too, interviewing anyone that knew Lauren. Lauren's neighbor and classmate Stephen McDaniel was more than happy to talk to reporters.

The strong summer breeze blew Stephen's long, messy curls into his face as he enthusiastically told television cameras that they had been looking for Lauren for the past four days. When asked what he thought may have happened to her, he hypothesized, "The only thing we can think of is that maybe she went out running and someone snatched her."

———

Thursday morning was garbage day. Just after 9:00 A.M., a trash truck arrived to empty the trash cans on the side of the apartment complex at Barrister Hall Apartments, but they had to skip the pickup because police cars blocked their access. If they had shown up any earlier police would have lost their biggest piece of evidence. At 9:40 A.M., police noticed a smell coming from a flip-top curbside plastic garbage can. When they laid the garbage can on its side and went through its contents, they found a black plastic garbage bag. Inside the bag was a female torso. The arms, legs, and head had been severed.

Stephen McDaniel was in the middle of a live interview with television news cameras when he got the news that police had found the torso. As he explained to the reporter where they had searched for Lauren that morning, the reporter asked, "What about in the parking lot area? I think that's where they've recovered a body." Stephen squinted as if he was confused. His face grew blank and he mumbled, "Body?"

The reporter continued asking him questions, but Stephen only stared wide-eyed with his mouth gaping open. He was unresponsive and rocked slightly side-to-side. The reporter asked, "Are you okay?" He looked as if he were on the verge of fainting and replied, "I think I need to sit down."

Stephen McDaniel Cries for the Nightly News Cameras

Stephen stumbled a few feet away and sat on the curb in a daze. Several minutes later, he returned to the television camera in tears. Crying hysterically, he told reporters he wished he could have helped her. He stuttered and stammered for almost ten minutes, saying that he wished he could have loaned her one of his guns. His performance, however, was a little over the top. It seemed overly extreme for someone that was only a neighbor and not a close friend. His interview caused investigators to take notice.

Throughout the day, police interviewed Lauren's friends and neighbors individually. Stephen McDaniel's interview started at 11:50 A.M. and he offered to help in any way he could. Right away, however, detectives noticed he was nervous and fidgety. His anxiety was a tell. Stephen had a scratch on his face. When police asked him to remove his shirt, there was another scratch on his stomach. He claimed he must have scratched himself as he slept. During the questioning, Stephen also made an odd comment. He claimed he was a virgin; saving himself for marriage.

Later in the day, the DNA from the torso had been compared to that of Lauren Gidding's mother and it was a match. The missing person case had just become a homicide and McDaniel became the prime suspect.

Stephen McDaniel had just graduated with a law degree. There was no question that he knew his rights. However, when investigators asked if they could search his apartment, he requested neither a warrant nor legal counsel. He simply agreed and led four investigators back to his apartment.

Inside his apartment, police found an extensive collection of swords and guns. Steven also had stockpiles of canned and dried foods and toilet paper, as if he were preparing for an apocalyptic lockdown. In a dresser drawer, police found a pair of women's underwear with holes cut into them – presumably so he could wear them as a mask.

As detectives continued their search of his apartment, Stephen dripped sweat profusely and drank ten bottles of water.

Detectives were puzzled when they found condoms in his nightstand drawer. Just hours earlier, Stephen had professed that he was a virgin and was saving himself for marriage. When asked why he had condoms, he told them he had stolen them from other apartments in the complex. In admitting that he had entered other apartments, he gave detectives exactly what they needed—probable cause to arrest him for burglary. Police brought Stephen McDaniel back to the police station for further interrogation while investigators continued searching his apartment.

On the ride back to the police station, Stephen's demeanor changed completely as he sat in the back of the squad car. He appeared as if he had some sort of mental breakdown. The entire ride, he sat quietly with a blank stare on his face and looked directly forward.

Once in the interrogation room, Stephen McDaniel spoke in a calm, robotic tone. "No." "I don't know." "I don't understand." Over and over, his answers were all the same. The young man that rambled to reporters for ten minutes just hours earlier now couldn't utter more than three words at a time.

His wide, unblinking eyes made him look as if he were in a permanently surprised state. They fixed directly into Detective Patterson's eyes, but seemed to look through him rather than at him. It almost appeared as if he were in some sort of trance. His responses to the barrage of questions were so monotone that at one point, Detective Patterson asked him if he had ever taken acid. His reply, of course, was a simple, "No."

It was well after midnight on the last day of June 2011.
Perhaps Stephen was just tired. After all, he had a long day.
Several days, actually. It was a lot of work dismembering a
human body.

Detective: "Why are you acting like this?"

Stephen: "I don't understand."

Detective: "Earlier today we sat here and talked, but now
you're acting like you don't know what's going on. Did
something happen to you? Why are you shutting down? Why
are you not talking to me?"

Stephen: "I don't know."

Detective: "Are you scared?"

Stephen: "No."

Stephen McDaniel Interrogation

Each answer was slow and deliberate, with his eyes never leaving the eyes of the detective. He remained distant and disengaged the entire time.

Two detectives took turns aggressively questioning him with little success. At one point, one detective used what's called the "futility technique." It was a technique where the interrogator plays on the doubts that are already present in the suspect's mind in an attempt to persuade them to admit guilt.

> Detective: "There's blood in your apartment, Stephen. You didn't get it up! Don't you watch CSI? Yeah, we know it. Stephen, why is there blood in your bathroom?"

The technique, however, had no effect on him because the detective was lying and Stephen knew it. He knew they wouldn't find blood in his apartment because he butchered her in her own apartment, not his.

When asked why he had so many guns, including a semi-automatic rifle, Stephen claimed he just liked them and had never fired them. Not once.

After two hours of an extremely strange interrogation (available in the online appendix at the end of this book), detectives let him speak to his mother, who had traveled to Macon to see him. When his mother entered the interrogation room, his demeanor changed back to the normal Stephen. His dazed answers were all for show – a pathetic strategy he had hoped would make him look insane.

The interrogation was useless, but investigators had gathered more than enough evidence at the scene to arrest Stephen McDaniel for murder.

In his apartment, police found a flash drive with hundreds of personal photos of Lauren Giddings. Some photos had been taken inside her apartment. They found a video camera with video taken from outside of Lauren's second-story window. He had attached the video camera to the end of a six-foot wooden pole. Stephen stood on the ground beneath her bedroom window and raised the camera up to record inside her bedroom. He recorded one video in the evening just before she was murdered.

Stephen had in his possession a master key to every apartment in the complex that he had stolen from a security guard whom had previously worked there. One of the most crucial pieces of evidence was a hacksaw that was found in a storage cabinet of the laundry room. There was still blood on the blade that contained Lauren Gidding's DNA. They found the packaging for the same blade in his apartment.

Searches of his computer's browser history showed Google searches for the terms "escape prison" and "choked unconscious how long wake up." The searches were entered just minutes before Lauren was murdered. Stephen's Facebook and LinkedIn histories had shown several visits to Lauren's online profiles. He had also visited websites and watched videos of sex with dead bodies and violent pornography.

———

With his bond set at $2.5 million, Stephen McDaniel sat in jail for the next three years while prosecutors built their case against him. The evidence continued to mount against him and he faced the death penalty. A death penalty trial could have taken five to seven years to prepare for, but in April 2014, Stephen saved the state those years and confessed to killing Lauren Giddings.

In a written statement Stephen admitted that on the night of June 26, 2011, around 4:30 A.M., he entered her apartment with the master key. Wearing gloves and a mask, he crept into her bedroom and stood in the doorway, watching her sleep. But when he took another step, the floorboard creaked and Lauren woke up. She yelled, "Get the fuck out!"

Stephen leapt onto her bed and wrapped his gloved hands around her throat. They fought and tumbled out of the bed and onto the floor. During the altercation, Lauren scratched his face and stomach. When she grabbed at his face, she pulled his mask off and realized it was Stephen. She cried, "Stephen? Please stop."

On the floor at the side of the bed, Lauren got her legs caught underneath the bed, which kept her from kicking him. Stephen sat on top of her and strangled her for fifteen minutes before she stopped moving.

Once she was dead, Stephen dragged her body into her bathroom, put her in the bathtub, and went back to his own apartment. He stayed in his apartment on his computer for almost twenty hours.

Just before midnight on Sunday night, Stephen returned to Lauren's apartment with a hacksaw. He removed her arms, legs, and head, placing them in black plastic garbage bags. He walked across the street to the Mercer Law School and placed the extremities in a dumpster. His mask, gloves, and the shirt he was wearing were cut into small pieces which he flushed down the toilet.

After dumping the body parts, Stephen returned to Lauren's apartment to clean up. He had contained the mess to the bathroom only.

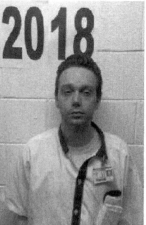

Stephen McDaniel

Stephen explained to detectives that he did not sexually assault her. He told that he didn't even take off her clothes and her torso still had on the same pink running shorts he had killed her in.

He went on to explain that he continued to prepare for the bar exam on Monday and attended a Bar prep class on Tuesday and Wednesday.

Stephen claimed that while he searched with Lauren's friends on Thursday, he was in a, "dream-like delusional state."

> "I believed, at the time, while taking part in the search, that Lauren was still alive and that I had not done what I had done, even searching the empty law school in a delusional hope of finding Lauren alive and well, as if I had not really killed her."

Stephen McDaniel expressed his sorrow and regret in the signed confession, but his shallow words did nothing to alleviate the grief experienced by Lauren's family.

Stephen chalked his actions up to momentary confusion and panic. He claimed he never intended on killing her, but his calculated actions showed premeditation. He had purchased the hacksaw blade days before he actually killed Lauren.

The fact was, Stephen McDaniel was a stalker and a voyeur. Plain and simple. The object of his obsession had graduated and was moving away within days, meaning she would no longer be in his life. It was his last chance. Stephen McDaniel couldn't bear the thought of never seeing Lauren Giddings again. Once she left school, he would just be someone she used to know. By murdering her, his actions connected them forever.

Stephen McDaniel was sentenced to life without the possibility of parole until 2041. The head, arms, and legs of Lauren Giddings were never recovered.

I FOUND MOM!

J ust after Labor Day in 1985, forty-two-year-old Leonard Tyburski was excited about the new school year. Summer had just come to a close, classes had begun, and he was getting to know his new students. The prior year he had been promoted to dean of students and chief disciplinary officer at Mackenzie High School, in the eastern suburbs of Detroit. Leonard had worked for the Detroit School District for over twenty years and in only a few more years he could retire.

Leonard met Dorothy Barker when he was twenty-one and working as a biology teacher. She was a sixteen-year-old sophomore in his class that had a crush on her handsome teacher. Her persistent flirting was more than he could resist and the two began a romantic relationship. Although they were only five years apart in age, a student-teacher romantic relationship violated school policy. For a time, they hid their taboo relationship, but they didn't want to live like that. With Leonard's promise of love and financial support, Dorothy dropped out of high school so they could keep the love affair alive.

Dorothy & Leonard Tyburski

After three years of dating, in 1967 Dorothy was of legal age and married Leonard. Dorothy's family didn't approve of the relationship from the very beginning. They knew Leonard and Dorothy weren't a good fit. Leonard was a controlling young man that didn't want his wife to work. He was old-fashioned and obsessed with cleanliness and order. In his eyes, a woman's job was to keep the house spotless; so that's exactly what she did.

Leonard did his best to keep Dorothy to himself and away from her family. He often intercepted phone calls from family members, telling them, "she's not here," or, "she's busy doing her chores." Her family members had their suspicions about abuse in the relationship early on when they noticed occasional bruises on Dorothy's arms. Once she showed up to visit with a black eye. However, Dorothy always had an excuse, so they never really knew for sure.

Dorothy and Leonard's first daughter, Kelly, was born after three years of marriage. Three years later came their second daughter, Kim. As far back as the girls could remember, there were constant arguments, objects being thrown across the room, pushing, screaming, and name-calling. Kim did her best to avoid the confrontations. She retreated to her bedroom and rarely came out. She had her own television, telephone, stereo, and even kept food in her room. Kelly, however, found herself in the middle of the disputes, usually taking her mother's side.

Dorothy was a sociable young woman who liked to chat with everyone. Her friendly demeanor made Leonard jealous and he often told the girls that their mother was having affairs with other men. When Dorothy was in her late twenties, he accused her of having an affair with a sixty-five-year-old pet shop owner. "There are others too," he would tell the girls; a man that she bred rabbits with, while another was the local pharmacist. Whether there was any truth to his accusations, the girls were never certain.

Leonard and Dorothy owned an attractive, ranch-style home in a nice neighborhood in suburban Detroit. She kept the home and yard immaculate, but that wasn't enough. Although Leonard's career was doing well, seventeen years of marriage had taken its toll and their relationship was quickly spiraling down the drain.

In 1984, Dorothy's sister, Lorraine, died in a car crash. Lorraine had been her best friend throughout her life and the two shared everything. The loss devastated Dorothy. Leonard, however, never appreciated the relationship between the two women. He knew Dorothy talked to her sister behind his back. When Lorraine died, he had no sympathy for his wife and her loss. He seemed happy about it because he could have his wife all to himself. As a result, Dorothy fell in to a deep depression. She wrote somber poetry and penned heartbreaking letters to her dead sister.

The following year, Kelly turned seventeen and Kim four-teen. The girls were teenagers and had lives of their own – lives outside of the home. Thirty-seven-year-old Dorothy felt alone and lethargic. Bored with her suburban life, she felt as if she had missed out on so much by dropping out of high school and marrying so young.

Throughout 1985, Dorothy and Leonard argued most of the time they were together, but the problems in the Tyburski household took an uncomfortable turn for the worse when Kelly started dating a new boy, Craig Albright. Craig and Kelly had worked together at the local Hardee's fast-food restaurant. He was an attractive, muscled, young eighteen-year-old and when Kelly brought him home to meet her parents, Dorothy took an instant liking to the boy. Perhaps Craig was the type of boy she wished she had dated when she was Kelly's age.

Each time Craig came to the house to visit Kelly, Dorothy made herself available. Kelly noticed a conspicuous change in her mother's behavior. Dorothy chatted endlessly with the young couple and unashamedly invited herself to tag along on their dates, often going to movies and restaurants with them. Suddenly, the couple had become a threesome, but the relationship between Kelly and her mother deteriorated. Dorothy became possessive of the young man and would get upset at Kelly if Craig didn't come over to visit.

Leonard noticed the drastic change in Dorothy as well. Their constant arguing had come to a pinnacle and Dorothy didn't seem to hide her attraction to Craig at all. In fact, she was shoving it in Leonard's face. She taunted him every chance she could.

When Craig had problems at his own home, his parents kicked him out of the house. Dorothy jumped at the opportunity to help and suggested he move in with them. He could stay on the couch until he could find another place to live. Leonard reluctantly agreed. Immediately after moving in, however, Craig noticed the simmering tension in the house. Leonard often yelled at Dorothy or the girls in front of him as if he weren't there.

Over the following three weeks, Dorothy aggressively pursued the young man. She ran around the house in her underwear, begging him to touch her. "Come on! Are you chicken?" Though she hid her advances from her daughter, she didn't care one bit if Leonard saw. She wanted him to see.

Eventually, Leonard approached Kelly and accused her mother of sleeping with Craig. Although she had her suspicions and had noticed her mother clinging to her boyfriend, Kelly swept the accusation aside. Craig would never do that to her. Her mother would never do that to her.

But it didn't take long for the boy to give in to the sexual advances of thirty-seven-year-old Dorothy. After a long day at the Michigan State Fair, Dorothy, Kelly, and Craig stopped the car in a parking lot to get some rest. As Kelly slept in the front seat, Dorothy quietly climbed into the back seat and had sex with Craig. They had sex an additional time at the Tyburski home, but Craig felt guilty for sleeping with his girlfriend's mother. When Dorothy propositioned him a third time, he turned her down.

Dorothy didn't take the rejection well. When Kelly came home from work on the evening of September 22, 1985, she found her mother at the kitchen table writing something on a piece of paper. Her father sat in the family room silently brooding. There was noticeable tension in the air, but they weren't speaking. When Kelly asked her mother what was going on, she replied,

> "I have something I want you to sign when I'm done. I took a bunch of pills and I'm going to die."

Kelly started crying hysterically and screamed at her father to call an ambulance. Unfazed, he rolled his eyes and didn't move.

When Dorothy finished writing, she pushed the paper in front of Kelly. It was an impromptu Last Will & Testament stating that she wanted the insurance money that she had inherited after her sister's death to be placed into a trust. She specifically wanted the trust to be controlled by her friend Linda. Not by Leonard. It also stated that Leonard was the fault of her suicide.

Kelly screamed at her mother and screamed at her father, but it was no use. The young girl felt she was somehow to blame for her mother's anguish. Kelly ran across the street to their neighbor Linda's house and pounded on the door. Kelly explained the situation to Linda, who initially thought it was a joke, but she soon realized the seriousness of the situation and called 911.

When Kelly returned to the house, Dorothy had disappeared and Leonard had made no effort to stop her from leaving. He still sat in the living room, undisturbed. Police and paramedics found her a half-mile away, passed out in a bank parking lot.

An ambulance rushed Dorothy to the hospital to have her stomach pumped. When she regained consciousness, Kelly and Craig visited her in the hospital room. Dorothy told Kelly she loved her and kissed her on the cheek, but when

Craig bent down to hug her, she kissed him full on the lips. Craig was markedly surprised and felt uncomfortable at the gesture. Kelly stood dumbfounded and realized that her mother was obsessed with her teenage boyfriend.

———

Four days later, Craig Albright was in the driveway of the Tyburski's home washing his car when Leonard came outside to speak to him. Leonard asked him to leave for thirty minutes or so because he needed to have a discussion with Dorothy. Craig knew that meant they were going to have another argument. Craig got in his car and went for a long drive.

Leonard walked back into the house and confronted Dorothy as she prepared dinner. He was sure she was having an affair and accused her of having sex with Craig, who was almost half her age. Defiantly, Dorothy admitted her affair and screamed at Leonard,

"I love him! Craig's a man! You're not!"

Leonard's blood boiled and he flew into a rage, but Dorothy continued to taunt him,

"You're just a wimp. A punk! You can't satisfy me like he can!"

Dorothy's emasculating comments continued as she headed down the stairs into the basement to get meat out of the freezer for dinner. At the bottom of the stairs, the couple continued to scream at each other. Dorothy told Leonard,

"I want you out of the house. I don't love you anymore. You need to move out!"

Leonard slapped her and she took a swing at him with the butcher's knife she had carried from the kitchen.

Leonard's mind exploded in anger as he grabbed her head and slammed it into the metal pillar that supported the home. The first blow knocked her unconscious, but he continued to beat her head against it over and over. He smashed her head into the post eleven times—until she slumped on the floor covered in blood.

In a stupor of what he had done, Leonard walked back up the stairs to his bedroom, washed up, and changed his clothes. All the while thinking that maybe when he went back down the stairs, she'd be fine. Maybe it had never happened. But it did. He went back into the basement, opened the chest freezer, dropped her body on top of the frozen hamburger and kielbasa, and twisted the lock.

———

When Craig returned to the house an hour later, Leonard met him in the driveway. Leonard was furious.

"Get the fuck out of here! Dorothy took off and you're not welcome here! Don't come back!"

Craig, of course, assumed correctly that Leonard had found out about his tryst with his wife.

"Shit, just let me get my clothes."

Leonard replied,

"If you step a foot in that house, I'll fucking kill you!"

Frustrated, Craig punched the side mirror of his own car, gouging his arm, before he climbed back into his car and drove off.

Craig drove to the Hardee's where Kelly had been working. He was so flustered he could barely speak.

> "Your mom and dad got into another fight or something. He kicked me out and won't even let me into the house to get my clothes. I think he thinks something's going on between me and your mom. And your mom's gone."

Just then, the phone at Hardee's rang. It was Leonard.

> "Don't talk to Craig! I don't want you hanging around him! Your mother and I got into a fight. I need you to come home right now and then go to Grandma's."

Kelly had never heard her father that angry. Too scared to speak to him, Kelly picked up Kim and went straight to their grandmother's house.

***

Right away, Leonard began spreading the seeds of Dorothy's mysterious disappearance. Just minutes after killing her, he walked across the street to Linda's house and told her that Dorothy had been having an affair with Craig Albright and she'd left him. In the following days, he told Dorothy's family that she had run off with another man and was living on a houseboat in Monroe, Michigan or Toledo, Ohio.

Dorothy's family had their doubts about Leonard's story—as did Kelly. At Kelly's insistence, Leonard reluctantly filed a missing person report with the Canton police four days after the incident. But when Kelly read the newspaper account of the police report, it confused her why her father told the police that Kim was the last person to see her mother. The article also said that Dorothy had a history of leaving home. Kelly knew that neither of those statements were true. Leonard told Kelly that he had watched Dorothy go out the door. The article also mentioned that Dorothy left with a large sum of money. Kelly knew, however, that her father never let Dorothy carry more than $30 or $40 at a time.

Police were suspicious of Leonard's explanation, but when he passed a lie-detector test, they wrote it off as just another woman leaving her husband.

Kelly and Craig had stopped dating in the days after Dorothy went missing. Over the following months, Kelly fell into a depression. Not because of the breakup, but because she somehow blamed herself for her mother's disappearance. Leonard had encouraged her self-imposed blame by telling her he had spoken to her mother, who told him she didn't want to speak to her daughters. "She told me she's mad at you."

To pacify Dorothy's family and daughters, Leonard had claimed that Dorothy had called him, asking him to bring her some clothes. He claimed he met her at a rest area just south of Detroit and brought her the clothes she asked for.

Again, Kelly had her suspicions. Kelly knew Kim left for school every day after her father left for work – and she got back from school before him as well. Kim rarely left the house. She would have known if her mother had called.

As the months passed, Kelly enrolled in school ninety miles away at Michigan State University. Not a day passed that she hadn't thought of her mother and why she hadn't called. Even if she had met another man, why hadn't she called her daughters or her own brother and sister? Why would she have missed Kelly's high school graduation? The unanswered questions haunted her.

Leonard worked hard to pit his two daughters against one another. Kim, still living at home, kept quiet, spending most of her time in her bedroom. To reward her, he showered her with gifts like a $1,500 drum set she kept in the basement—without knowing it was just a few feet from her mother's frozen body. Kelly, however, was still inquisitive. Leonard often complained of how much her schooling was costing him and protested every time she called home. He had to pay the long-distance phone bill.

By the fall of 1988, Kelly's depression worsened. She couldn't eat or sleep and had lost over twenty pounds. When she managed to sleep, she often dreamt of her mother. In her dreams, she saw her mother silently hunched over in a chair. Kelly would try to run to her, but she couldn't move. In her dreams, she could sense that her mother was mad.

Over the Thanksgiving holiday, Kelly went home to spend the holiday with Kim and her father. During her stay, Kelly cooked for the family and went down to the basement freezer. Kelly loved the stuffed cabbage that her mother used to make and it was something she had often served for Thanksgiving dinner. Maybe her mother had left some in the freezer. But when Kelly reached for the key to the freezer that usually hung on a hook on the wall, it was missing.

When she asked her father where the key was, his response was, "Your mother took it when she left." An odd response, Kelly thought. Why on earth would her mother leave without clothes, but take the key to the chest freezer?

Kelly returned to finish the year at school, then returned home again the following month for Christmas break. Although they no longer dated, Kelly still kept in touch with Craig Albright. When he heard she was in town for the winter break, he invited her to a New Year's Eve party.

At the party, Kelly told Craig about the dreams of her mother and the strange incident with the freezer key. She said something just didn't seem right about the freezer being locked for three and a half years. Why wouldn't her father have just popped the lock off? It all seemed very strange. Craig agreed and suggested, "Why don't you just get a screw driver and pry it open?" Kelly jokingly replied, "Yeah, Dad probably put her in there, right?"

———

On January 2, 1989, Kelly was packing her bag to return to school, but all she could think of was the conversation she had with Craig about the freezer. Kelly crept down the basement stairs and stared at the lock on the freezer. Craig's suggestion stuck in her head. She paused a beat, then searched her father's nearby toolbox and pulled out a large screwdriver and a paint lid remover.

Upstairs, Kim sat in her bedroom and could hear loud pounding coming from the basement. Leonard had gone to an electronics store to buy a new set of stereo speakers, so she knew the banging wasn't coming from her father. Moments later, she heard the fast "thud, thud, thud" of someone running up the basement stairs. Kelly burst into Kim's room and screamed,

"Oh my God! Mom's in the freezer! Mom's in the freezer!"

"What?!"

"I found Mom in the freezer!"

Both of their hearts pounded with fear and shock. Leonard was due home any minute. The girls knew that if their father saw they had opened the freezer, they might end up just like their mother. Moments later, Leonard walked in the back door. Restraining themselves, the girls remained composed as they spoke to their father for the next several minutes.

———

Craig had planned to drive Kelly back to school that afternoon and arrived an hour after the girls had found their mother's body. As Craig walked into the house, Kelly whispered, "Act like nothing has happened."

"Why?" He whispered back.

"Because I just found mom," she replied.

Kelly and Kim got into the car and Craig drove to the police station. They didn't want to be anywhere near the house when the police arrived.

———

Leonard Tyburski was arrested and charged with murder. He confessed to killing his wife. He claimed they were arguing, she went down the stairs to get something out of the freezer, and he followed. She had a kitchen butcher's knife in one hand and a fork in the other. She swung the knife at him, then threw it at him, all the while shouting emasculating remarks.

"She kept yelling and saying that Craig satisfied her, and I didn't. And she kept looking at me and calling me a wimp, a punk, and a bastard."

Leonard explained he flew into a rage and slammed her head into the vertical metal support beam. He then claimed that Dorothy stumbled backwards and fell into the freezer.

Leonard Tyburski / The Chest Freezer

Leonard told detectives she fell half-in, half-out of the freezer, but she was still breathing and conscious. He then went upstairs and washed the blood off of himself. When he came back downstairs, she was dead.

Detectives easily disproved his story. Dorothy's head had been smashed eleven times, which would have easily killed her. She also had a broken index finger, defensive wounds on her forearms, and multiple bruises on her face, chest, and shoulders.

Because there was no evidence of premeditation, the judge ruled that the prosecution was limited to a charge of manslaughter or second-degree murder. Leonard Tyburski was charged and convicted of second-degree murder and sentenced to twenty to forty years in prison. In November 1994, however, his conviction was overturned on a technicality. Rather than go through another trial, Tyburski pleaded guilty in exchange for a reduced sentence. After serving only ten years, Leonard Tyburski was released from prison.

After his release, Leonard Tyburski returned to his childhood home in Monessen, Pennsylvania, to live with his elderly parents. In interviews with the press, Tyburski said,

> "I went through hell. That was a bad part of my life. I want to forget about it. People commit crimes and are punished for it. I've paid for what I did."

He lived off of his Detroit School District pension until his death in 2014.

Kim Tyburski stuck by her father's side during his trial, prison sentence, and afterward. Kelly, however, was much less supportive. In the years after his release, Kelly warmed up to him somewhat, but only described her relationship with her father as, "fine."

3

LIKE MOTHER, LIKE SON

Ninety miles east of New York City is home to the Pocono Mountains, a majestic area that's a popular year-around vacation spot for New Yorkers. The vast mountains, lakes, streams, and woods make it a perfect place for everything from fishing and boating to mountain biking, skiing, and golfing.

The Kunkle family had deep roots in the Poconos, dating back to the early German and Pennsylvania Dutch immigrants. In the center of Monroe County was a small village named Kunkletown that got its name from Joseph Kunkle, one of the first successful business owners in the area almost 200 years ago.

Cheryl Kunkle was born in 1969 and raised in the area by her father, who ran a junkyard that sold scrap metal and reusable car parts. Growing up at the junkyard gave Cheryl a rough exterior that made her into a tomboy. She playing baseball, worked on cars, rode a motorcycle, and was every bit as tough as any boy in the small town.

In 1986, at just seventeen, Cheryl found herself pregnant and dropped out of school to take care of the baby she named Gregory Rowe. Before his first birthday, however, Cheryl had grown tired of Greg's father, Jeffrey Rowe, and the couple broke up.

Cheryl didn't want to be with Jeffrey, but she also didn't want him to be with anyone else. When he started dating another woman, Cheryl became spiteful and refused to let him see his son. As a result, Greg spent his childhood believing that his father wanted nothing to do with him. The truth, however, was that his mother was keeping Greg and his father apart. Some of Jeffrey's relatives didn't even know he had a son because Cheryl had refused to let them see each other.

Cheryl was an angry, overbearing mother that was critical of every move Greg made throughout his life. She associated him with his father, whom she despised. She saw Jeffrey's face every time she looked at Greg.

Her relatives grew accustomed to Cheryl dropping Greg off at their doorstep without notice anytime she had an errand to run. Greg grew up feeling that his Aunt Cindy was more of a mother figure than his real mother was.

Cheryl was a hard worker, though. She spent years working manual labor jobs that were typically more suitable for men; a welder, construction, and a forklift driver in a warehouse. Eventually she started her own paving business, laying blacktop on roads and parking lots. The work paid well. Cheryl bought a house and drove a Mercedes. It made her happy thinking that maybe she had shed the image of being from the "junkyard family."

———

Ben Amato moved to the Poconos from New York City in the mid-nineties. The forty-seven-year-old had retired from the New York Sanitation Department, where he had worked as a truck mechanic. The Poconos offered what he considered a relaxed retirement. He started a snowplow business, worked as a volunteer firefighter, and fixed up vintage cars. While looking for car parts, Ben would often rummage through Cheryl's father's junkyard.

Although he was almost twenty years older than twenty-eight-year-old Cheryl, she saw stability in Ben and started flirting with him. Ben was more than receptive and the two started dating. Though she was rough, Ben was excited to have a younger woman so interested in him. Best of all, he got along well with twelve-year-old Greg.

Cheryl Kunkle & Ben Amato

Over the next several months, Ben showered Greg with gifts and more expensive gifts for Cheryl. He was in love and perhaps she was too, but it all changed when Cheryl realized she was pregnant with Ben's child.

Her demeanor instantly shifted and she stopped answering his phone calls without notice. After repeated attempts to reach her, she finally broke the news to Ben. It was over. Suddenly, she wanted nothing to do with him. She planned to keep the child, but wanted to raise it on her own and didn't want him involved at all. Cheryl broke off all contact.

Ben spiraled into a deep depression. It wasn't just the loss of his love, Cheryl, but the loss of the son he would never meet. The once happy-go-lucky man had become reclusive and private. He wouldn't speak to any of his friends and family about his situation, instead keeping his feelings hidden inside.

Cheryl gave birth to her second boy in November 1998, giving him the surname Kunkle instead of his father's name, Amato. Meanwhile, Ben saw therapists that prescribed him anti-depressants. A year later, he attempted suicide and failed. He tried again the following year. His friends and family were at a loss for what they could do.

Similar to Jeffrey Rowe, Cheryl had pushed Ben aside and denied any contact with his son. Over time, however, Ben seemed to emerge from his depression. He decided he would fight Cheryl for custody of their son—but Cheryl fought dirty.

She assumed that if she filed harassment charges against Ben before the custody hearing, the judge would look poorly upon him in court. Cheryl charged that Ben had been stalking her ever since he decided he wanted to share custody of the boy. The judge, however, saw through her charade and told Cheryl,

> "Just because he drives past your house doesn't mean he's stalking you."

Cheryl startled the judge when she blurted,

> "What do I have to do to get him to leave me alone? Do I
> have to fucking kill him?!"

Although she said it on a whim, Cheryl wasn't joking. In
August 2001, she asked her friend April Steinhauser if she
knew someone that could "knock off my ex-boyfriend for
$5000?" April quickly replied, "Yes, I do!" Cheryl knew April
was a crack cocaine addict and was likely to hang around the
type of people that could arrange a murder-for-hire. April
told her she wouldn't have to look far—her boyfriend Nate
Evans could do the job.

Cheryl met with Nate to arrange the hit, but during their
discussions, Cheryl couldn't decide how she wanted the job
done. She told him to shoot him inside his house, or follow
him home and shoot him as he got out of his truck. The
more she thought about it, however, Cheryl realized it would
be best to make it look like an accident – or better yet, a
suicide. Ben had already attempted suicide twice; it would be
believable. Cheryl gave Nate a photo of Ben and drew him
the layout of his house.

When Cheryl opened her safe to pay Nate, she rethought her
original $5,000 price. It was too much. She offered him
$3,000 instead. $1,500 now, then the rest when the job is
done. In his mind, Nate had already spent the money on his
and April's next fix. He quickly took whatever Cheryl
offered.

Nate, however, was no killer. Neither was April. They were
only interested in the money and after seeing Cheryl open
her safe, their motivation changed. A few days after the

initial meeting, Nate and April broke into Cheryl's house and stole from her safe, which held an additional $6,500.

When Cheryl realized her safe had been stolen, she was livid and reported it to the police. She told them exactly who to look for: Nathaniel Evans and April Steinhauser. But before police could question them, Cheryl confronted Nate, demanded her money back, and threatened to press charges. Nate, however, replied,

> "Don't forget... I'm the guy you paid to murder your ex-boyfriend."

Cheryl knew that if she pressed charges against Nate and April, they could drag her down with them. Cheryl called the police and told them she wanted to drop the charges against Nate and April.

———

Three months later, in early November 2001, Ben Amato's neighbors noticed his two dogs had been on his front porch for several days, but they hadn't seen Ben. His neighbors knew he had battled depression for the past three years and worried that he may have attempted suicide one more time. They called the police to do a welfare check.

When police arrived, they found Ben at the bottom of his basement stairs. He was face-down in a pool of his own blood. At first look, police believed Ben had fallen down the flight of stairs, hit his head, and died, but an autopsy and forensic examination of the scene proved otherwise.

The medical examiner determined Ben had been dead for five days before they found his body. They found pepper spray on his face and on the walls at the top of the stairs. Ben had died of blunt force trauma, but not from the fall. Someone had repeatedly beaten him on the head with a large cylindrical object. But the most telling piece of evidence was a boot print at the bottom of the stairs. Someone had stepped in his blood pool while it was fresh and tracked it on the basement floor.

When Ben's stepdaughter heard of his death, she knew it had to be the work of Cheryl Kunkle. He and Cheryl were just weeks away from a child custody hearing and he seemed to be overcoming his depression. His stepdaughter wasn't the only one that suspected Cheryl. The judge that presided over Cheryl's harassment charge, Debby York, alerted detectives of what Cheryl had said in court, "What do I have to do to get him to leave me alone? Do I have to fucking kill him?!"

———

Though suspicion clearly pointed toward Cheryl, detectives had no physical evidence that pointed directly to her. Cheryl often wore work boots, but the bloody boot print didn't match any boots in her possession.

Two years had passed with no new clues or an arrest in the case. There was still one thing that puzzled investigators— the burglary accusation that Cheryl suddenly dropped three months before Ben's death. Cheryl had accused Nate Evans of the burglary, but she mysteriously withdrew the charge. Detectives wanted to know why.

Nate Evans had been arrested on an unrelated charge and was sitting in jail at the time of Ben Amato's death. He couldn't have done it. Detectives met with Nate in jail, sat him down, and asked, "Do you know why we're here?" Nate's reply shocked them, "Yeah, you're here about us getting paid by that lady to kill that dude."

Nate and April both told police that Cheryl had paid them to kill Ben Amato, but they had no intention of following through. They were only interested in stealing her money and said they used the money to buy new bicycles for April's daughters. They spent any remaining cash on drugs and alcohol. The new information wasn't enough to arrest Cheryl for murder, but they could at least arrest her for solicitation to commit murder. Cheryl Kunkle sat in jail for several months, but eventually raised money for bail and was released awaiting trial.

―――――

For the next year and a half, detectives built a case against Cheryl but hoped that additional evidence would present itself so they could arrest her for Ben's murder. Detectives would get their murder charge, but not in the manner they had hoped.

―――――

Cheryl's son, Greg Rowe, was seventeen in 2003 and lived with his mother and his younger brother. He worked laying blacktop for Cheryl's company and had been dating a sixteen-year-old local girl named Kristin Fisher. However, Greg and Kristin's relationship had fallen apart when Kristin became pregnant with their child. Rowe refused to acknowledge that the baby was his. He demanded she have an abortion, but Kristin refused. She had made up her mind and was planning to raise the baby with or without him. In October

2003, Kaylee Elizabeth Fisher was born, but Rowe wanted nothing to do with the little girl.

Kristin & Kaylee Fisher / Gregory Rowe

By early May 2004, Greg and Kristin were embroiled in a legal battle. Just as Cheryl had suspected, Kristin had filed a domestic relations complaint against Greg and was suing for child support. Cheryl attended mediation with her son before he and Kristin went to court. Cheryl was cold and angry. She pointed at Kaylee across the table and snarled at Kristin, "Is that really his? I don't think it's his!"

Kristin and her mother, Kathleen, spoke on the phone the morning of May 4. The child support hearing was scheduled for the following afternoon and Kristin told her mother, "Greg is on his way over. He said he has a surprise for me and Kaylee." Kathleen was worried. "Don't let him in the house," she warned. "You know what he's capable of!" But Kristin told her mother it was too late—Greg had just arrived, and not to worry.

Kathleen arrived home at 5:30 P.M. that evening and opened the garage door to find Kristin on the garage floor. A thin white rope tied into a noose hung loosely around her neck. The other end of the rope was attached to the garage door opener railings. An overturned stool laid nearby. Kathleen ran to her daughter, but it was far too late. She was cold. Frantically, Kathleen rushed into the house, looking for Kaylee. She ran from room to room, but there was no sign of the baby. She was troubled by the lack of crying. Had Greg taken Kaylee? But when Kathleen entered the downstairs bathroom, she collapsed to her knees. Her seven-month-old granddaughter was lifeless, face-down in the half-filled bathtub.

When police arrived, it was obvious someone had staged the scene to look as if Kristin had killed her daughter and committed suicide. The noose was loose around her neck, certainly not tight enough to have killed her. Also, the tops of her feet were dirty, but the bottoms were clean - an indication that someone had dragged her into the garage. An autopsy confirmed that she had been strangled rather than hanged.

Typically Kristin wore sweatpants around the house, but she was dressed in her street clothes and the diaper bag was packed, indicating she was planning on leaving the house. Generally, it wasn't something someone would do before drowning their own baby and committing suicide.

When police questioned neighbors, one man had noticed a Honda Civic parked in front of Kristin's house that day. He hadn't recognized the vehicle, thought it looked out of place, and had the foresight to write down the license plate number. When police checked the registration, the car was registered jointly to Greg Rowe and Cheryl Kunkle.

Police arrived with a warrant at Greg's home, where he was living with his mother. Cheryl was furious that police were rummaging through her house. When she went into the garage, detectives told her specifically not to go near the Honda Civic, but she brazenly ignored their commands. Cheryl was arrested for hindering apprehension, obstructing justice, and tampering with evidence. She claimed that she only wanted to get some CDs out of the car, but investigators believed she was trying to hide evidence.

Cheryl had been out on bail awaiting trial on her own murder investigation of Ben Amato. However, after the obstructing justice charge, they revoked her bail for the original charge and returned her to jail. Reporters watched as she entered the jail and asked her how she felt about her granddaughter's death. She angrily barked back at the reporter,

> "Granddaughter? That's not my granddaughter! My son was wearing a condom and the birth date does not make sense!"

During the sweep of the home, police collected Greg's computer hoping to find emails between himself and Kristin that would show problems in their relationship, but they found much more than they were looking for. Rowe's computer contained seven photos and two videos of child pornography. Police charged Rowe with nine counts of sexual abuse of children, nine counts of criminal attempt at dissemination, one count of criminal use of a computer, and nine counts of obscene or other sexual materials.

Despite the charges, Rowe was released after posting $10,000 bail, but remained the prime suspect in the murder of Kristin and Kaylee. Thirteen days later, Cheryl's hindering apprehension charge was dropped, but it wasn't enough to get her out of jail. She remained in custody, awaiting her trial for the solicitation to commit murder charge.

Over the next several weeks, detectives spoke to Kristin's friends and family. One friend claimed that just days before her death, Greg had left Kristin a message on her voicemail threatening to kill her if she didn't drop the child support lawsuit. Although investigators weren't able to retrieve a copy of the message, telephone records confirmed that Rowe had indeed called that day.

The neighbor that saw Greg's Honda Civic parked outside her house on the day of the murder provided an important piece of evidence. However, the most damning piece of evidence came from an employee at a nearby True Value Hardware store. The employee claimed Rowe came into the store on the day of the murder and purchased a bundle of thin white rope. The same type of rope found around Kristin's neck.

Rowe's freedom didn't last long. After little more than a month, he was charged with two counts of first-degree murder, two counts of third-degree murder, possessing instruments of crime, and endangering the welfare of children.

Cheryl Kunkle / Gregory Rowe

If convicted, Rowe faced the possibility of the death penalty. He insisted he did not kill his ex-girlfriend and daughter, but he knew who did. Rowe blamed his mother for the killings. He claimed that Cheryl not only killed Kristin and Kaylee, but she killed her boyfriend Ben Amato – and he could prove it.

———

Rowe laid out the scene for the prosecution. He told them that two months before Ben Amato's murder, he and his mother went to a sporting goods store where she told him to go inside and buy a can of bear repellant. The bear repellant later proved to be the pepper spray found on Ben's face and on the walls of the stairwell.

Then, on the day Ben Amato was murdered, he drove his mother to Ben's house. Despite being only fifteen years old, he regularly drove his mother around. He claimed he knew that she and Ben were in a child custody dispute and his mother instructed him to drive her to Ben's house. When they reached the house, Greg dropped her off and Cheryl told him to go about a mile away and wait for two hours. After two hours, he returned to the house.

When he picked his mother up at the house, he told prosecutors he had no idea what she had done. Cheryl was excited and seemed to be in an adrenaline rush. She instructed him to drive on the back roads on the way home. He said his mother climbed into the back seat of the car, removed her clothes, and threw them out the window as they drove through the rural roads. She also threw a blood-stained baseball bat out the window.

When Greg asked his mother what she had done, she confessed, "I killed him." She told him she sprayed Ben with the pepper spray at the top of the stairs and beat him with the baseball bat. As he stumbled down the stairs, she beat him more as he tried to fight her off. When he landed at the bottom of the stairs, she continued pummeling his head until he was dead.

Greg told detectives that when he found out what she had done, he was furious with his mother. He said he was only fifteen at the time and liked Ben. "I felt it was my fault. I cried and went to my bedroom."

Two days later, Cheryl was having second thoughts about her decision to throw her clothes and the murder weapon out the window of the car. She told Greg to go back and find them. Greg, however, claimed he wanted nothing to do with murdering Ben. He lied to his mother and told her he couldn't find them. She later asked another friend, Gerry, that she had admitted the murder to. Gerry refused to help her as well. Frustrated, Cheryl drove through the back roads on her own and found the items, brought them all home, and burned them.

Investigators believed his story about the Ben Amato murder, but didn't believe that Cheryl also killed Kristin and Kaylee. Far too many pieces of evidence pointed directly at Greg. They knew his car had been parked outside. He had made death threats to Kristin in the past and he purchased the same rope found around Kristin's neck.

During Greg Rowe's trial, his new girlfriend, Rachel Shavelson, testified against him. She told the court that just two days before Kristin and Kaylee were murdered, Greg had asked her to search the Internet for instructions on how to tie a hangman's noose.

Greg sent letters to Rachel from prison in which he told her to remember three things during her testimony. He wanted her to lie for him. He told her to testify that he bought the rope only at his mother's request and his mother had referred to Kristin as "business you should have taken care of yourself." Lastly, his letter asked her to testify that it was his mother that asked for the instructions on how to tie the noose, not himself. Rachel told the court that Greg repeatedly told her if she didn't say these things in court, his mother would kill her.

Greg's defense tried to blame the killings on Cheryl, but the jury didn't buy it. In January 2006, after six days of testimony and over five hours of deliberation, Greg Rowe was found guilty on two counts of first-degree murder and one count of third-degree murder.

Greg faced the death penalty. His father, Jeffrey Rowe, whom he had only recently reconciled with, addressed the court and pleaded for his son's life. He told the court that he had

no contact with Greg for years and was just getting to know
him again.

> "I know my son didn't do this. Please don't take him from
> me. I know two innocent lives were lost, but taking his life
> won't make it right."

Greg also pleaded with the jury,

> "I wanted to make my family proud of me. I know it's your
> opinion I did this, but I honestly tell you I didn't. Please
> don't take me from my family."

Ultimately, Greg Rowe was sentenced to life in prison
without the chance of parole.

———

The following year, in 2007, Greg Rowe was allowed outside
of the prison walls, but only to testify against his mother at her
trial. Wearing handcuffs, leg-restraints, and a black suit, Rowe
testified for two hours. He told the court that Cheryl admitted
to him she had killed Ben Amato and he had driven her to and
from the home that day. He claimed that his mother had
threatened him. She told him that if the police looked at her,
she would take him down with her as an accomplice.

Ben Amato's attorney and personal friend testified that Ben
told him repeatedly, "If I'm found dead, Cheryl did it." Debby
York, the judge that presided over Cheryl's harassment suit,
testified about Cheryl's death threat outburst.

At the time of the murder, Cheryl had been having an affair
with a married police officer, Marty Reynolds. Reynolds

took the stand to testify against her as well. He told the court that Cheryl had admitted to him she killed Ben, telling him, "We fought all the way down the stairs." She showed him the bruises on her thighs from the fight, then minutes later denied everything and told him the bruises were from a motorcycle accident.

"She was cuckoo. She was out there." Reynolds said Cheryl would say something one minute, then backtrack it a minute later.

Because Reynolds had withheld evidence about the murder, he was forced to resign from the police department where he had worked for almost ten years, his pension was revoked, and his wife divorced him.

Cheryl's close friend Gerry testified that she tried to get him to help find the baseball bat that she had thrown out of the car window. He also testified that he watched her burn the bat and her clothes. April Steinhauser also testified that Cheryl had paid her and her boyfriend to murder Ben.

Cheryl's defense admitted a cassette tape into evidence of a conversation between her and April, but the conversation was clearly staged, making her look even more guilty.

There wasn't much doubt of Cheryl's guilt. In February 2007, she was found guilty of first-degree murder. Four months later, she was sentenced to life in prison without the possibility of parole.

Ben Amato's stepdaughter and daughter addressed Cheryl Kunkle before she left the courtroom,

> "The prison you will be transferred to will have lots of prisoners like you. When you look into those many evil eyes,

may you finally see what my stepfather saw just before he took his last breath."

Ben's daughter continued,

"Last Sunday was Father's Day, and instead of taking my dad to dinner or having him over for a barbecue, I was sitting at a grave telling him 'Happy Father's Day,' and kissing a cold picture on a headstone."

As Cheryl left the courtroom, reporters asked her how she felt about spending the rest of her life in prison. She replied, "I don't intend to." In subsequent interviews from prison, Cheryl Kunkle still claims her innocence.

4

A HEARTLESS MOTHER

Paul Boehm had been working as a bus driver in St. Louis, Missouri, when he met eighteen-year-old Ellen Booker. Although he was married, his marriage was crumbling quickly. Ellen was young enough to be his daughter, but the attraction was too much for him to resist.

Ellen, too, felt an instant attraction despite Paul's age and marital status. She was at least one hundred pounds over-weight and Paul had been the first man to show any interest in her at all.

———

Growing up, Ellen had barely known her father. He had been an emotionally and physically abusive man, a heavy drinker, and had a short temper. It was probably a good thing that he was barely ever home. When she was still a young girl, her father left her mother, just as he had abandoned his previous wife and seven children. But when he died of cancer in 1979,

Ellen inherited one-eighth of the family farm and sold her share to her step-brother.

———

By the spring of 1978, Paul's first marriage had ended. Two years later, he married Ellen. Using her inheritance and his Veteran's benefits, they purchased the home they had been renting on Wyoming Street in St. Louis.

A few months after moving in, Ellen's mother, Christine, lost her job and Paul offered to let her move into the basement of their home. He assumed Ellen would like the idea of her mother so close, but he was wrong. Ellen had worked hard to create a life on her own and didn't want her mother so close. However, she realized that having Christine would come in handy, as they planned to create a family.

The family came quickly. Their daughter Jessica was born in September 1981. Four years later, Steven was born. Immediately after she gave birth to Steven, she became pregnant again with their second son, David.

———

Even before she had met Paul, Ellen Boehm had developed an obsession with professional wrestling. Not the kind of wrestling you'd see in the Olympics, but theatrical, choreographed wrestling featuring muscled men with names like Brutus Beefcake, Macho Man Randy Savage, and Hulk Hogan.

Initially, Paul attended the wrestling matches with Ellen, but couldn't quite understand her strange fixation on the silly sport. It was a relief for him when Ellen met Deanne Smith.

Deanne was an extreme fan of professional wrestling as well;
they were two peas in a pod. The two started attending
matches together, often traveling overnight just to see their
favorite wrestlers. This arrangement was fine with Paul, who
would rather spend his time and money drinking in bars.

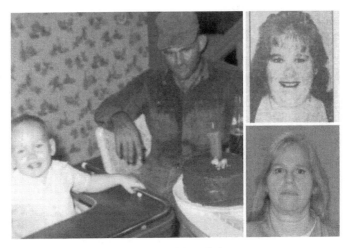

Ellen, Paul, and Steven Boehm

Ellen Boehm had returned from an overnight wrestling trip
with Deanne, just in time for her and Paul's sixth wedding
anniversary, when Paul gave her some bad news. During his
time in Vietnam, he had been exposed to agent orange; a
herbicidal warfare chemical that later caused major health
problems for those that had been exposed to it. As a result,
he often broke out in rashes all over his body. He told Ellen
that the military would cover his treatment, but he would
need to travel to Texas to stay in a military hospital. He
would have to quit his job because the treatment could take
several months. Ellen was eight months pregnant with David
when Paul left for Texas.

Deanne Smith was going through a difficult divorce at the time and thought it was odd that Paul's doctors hadn't consulted with Ellen before such a major treatment. It sounded suspicious. She suggested Ellen drive to the hospital and see if he had even parked his car there.

Initially, Ellen thought it was unlikely that Paul would have left her just a month before their third child was born. But after a few weeks without a word from Paul, she took Deanne's advice and drove to the hospital. Just as she had suggested, his car wasn't there.

Ellen was still in denial that her husband had left her, but when a former co-worker confirmed Paul had been having an affair with a young girl named Teri, she knew her marriage was over.

———

David Boehm was born in the summer of 1986 and Paul showed up at the maternity ward to play the part of the proud father. He held David in his arms and posed for a photo, but it would end up being the only time he ever saw his son. Two weeks later, Paul moved to Dodge City, Texas, with his new girlfriend, Teri. Ellen and Paul were divorced not long afterwards, then he married Teri.

Paul was on his third wife and had left Ellen the same way he'd left his previous wife. Ironically, this was the same way Ellen's own father had abandoned his two families.

After her divorce, Ellen immersed herself in professional wrestling. She and Deanne often traveled for long weekends to out-of-town events, sometimes following the wrestlers from town to town to watch the same choreographed shows every night.

Ellen had an active imagination. She often told friends and co-workers that she was having romantic relationships with the wrestlers. She developed an obsession with one wrestler in particular, Ted DiBiase, known as "The Million Dollar Man."

Every chance she got, she would desperately try to speak to DiBiase. She yelled to him as he walked down the aisle toward the ring on event nights and waited in the hotel bars where he stayed, hoping to get a chance to flirt with him.

She tried to flirt with many of the wrestlers, but at well over 300 pounds, none of them were interested in her. She threw herself at them, only to be rejected each time. The rejection, however, didn't keep her from fantasizing. She made up stories of torrid love affairs that she regularly shared with her friends. In Ellen's mind, the men couldn't resist her, when the truth was they wanted nothing to do with her. Ellen's obsession with wrestling was an unhealthy escape from reality.

Ellen worked a data entry job at an accounting firm, but it wasn't enough to make ends meet. She took a second job four nights a week delivering pizza in order to feed her kids and still be able to travel for wrestling matches.

Despite the extra job, however, it still wasn't enough and the bank foreclosed on the house that she had purchased with Paul. Ellen and her three kids moved into the Riverbend City Apartments along the banks of the Mississippi River. Although she couldn't afford to pay her mortgage, Ellen always found a few hundred dollars to spend every weekend on wrestling matches.

Ellen and Paul's divorce decree stated that Paul was obligated to pay monthly child support for his three children, but it didn't happen. Ellen never saw a dime. Still unable to pay the bills, she filed for bankruptcy in September 1987. Although it paid off her debts, her paychecks were being garnished and she was unable to pay her utilities.

Thanksgiving 1988 was busy for Ellen. After having a traditional Thanksgiving meal, she drove her three children into downtown St. Louis to see the department store window displays that had been decorated for Christmas.

Two-year-old David grew tired throughout the day and slept in the back of the car as she drove home. But by the time they arrived home that evening, just after 9:00 p.m., David was wide awake. He had gotten his second wind and wanted to watch television.

It was Ellen's night to watch her favorite show, Knot's Landing, and David wanted to watch too. Ellen sat on the sofa and David laid on the floor with a pillow to watch the show.

It's unclear what was going through Ellen's mind as she watched the show. Perhaps she contemplated the frustration she felt by raising three kids on her own or having Thanksgiving dinner without the love and support of a husband. Ellen moved from the couch and knelt on the floor, just behind David. As the boy watched television, she pulled a cushion from the couch, moved the boy onto his back, and placed the cushion over his face. She put her weight onto the edges of the cushion and held it tight across his face until his kicking and resistance stopped.

Ellen sat back down on the sofa while David lay unresponsive on the floor. His lips had turned a pale shade of blue. She calmly picked up the phone and called her friend Sandy—a friend she had known since high school. Ellen made small talk with Sandy and the two women discussed their Thanksgiving holiday. All the while, David lay at her feet, motionless.

After fifteen minutes of casual conversation, Ellen suddenly cut Sandy off. She told her that her son David was lying on the floor and had, just then, stopped breathing and was turning blue. Ellen explained she needed to hang up and call 911.

Several minutes later, paramedics arrived and pounded on the door, but there was no answer. They pounded again. Still nothing. Several minutes had passed when Jessica finally answered the door and explained that her mother had gone downstairs.

The paramedics entered the apartment to find David unresponsive on the floor. He was in cardiac arrest. Their initial attempts to revive him were unsuccessful and they prepared him for the ambulance.

After ten minutes, Ellen finally returned. She told the emergency team she had gone downstairs to find help. She seemed strangely calm and explained that David had been sick earlier in the day. Paramedics offered to let her ride in the ambulance with her son, but she declined. She said she would just meet them at the hospital.

When the paramedics left the apartment with David, Ellen called Sandy back and asked if she could watch the kids for the evening while she went to the hospital.

When David arrived at the emergency room, doctors were unable to resuscitate him and placed him on life-support. His body temperature reached 101 degrees and doctors used ice to keep the temperature down.

That evening, doctors thought it was strange that Ellen didn't stay by David's side throughout the night. Instead, she informed hospital staff that she would go back home to get some sleep and return in the morning.

The next morning, just after 9:00 A.M., Ellen returned to the hospital and told nurses she had "a good night's sleep." David's condition had not changed. From the hospital, Ellen called Deanne to tell her what had happened. Deanne rushed to the hospital to be by the side of her friend in her time of need, but she noticed Ellen didn't seem to be upset at all. Deanne was showing more emotion than Ellen. She assumed Ellen must have been up all night at David's bedside and was just in a state of shock and exhaustion.

After lunch, Ellen told Deanne she would take a nap in the waiting room and Deanne thought that was a good idea. She didn't know that Ellen had just had a full night's sleep. While Ellen slept, Deanne sat by David's bedside, rubbing his cold legs.

Deanne sat with David into the late evening and woke Ellen at 11:00 P.M., who was still asleep in the waiting room. She had slept the entire day. David's doctors had finished a brain scan, but the boy's brain was showing no activity at all.

Late that night as they drove home, Deanne noted that Ellen still didn't seem to be that upset about David's condition and said, "You must have been exhausted having stayed up all night with David." She was astonished to hear Ellen admit she had gone home and slept the night before.

Deanne stayed with Ellen that night. In the morning Deanne called the hospital, but the news wasn't good. David had shown no signs of recovery. When they arrived back at the hospital, Ellen lifted David's eyelids, looking for any reaction at all. Nothing.

That afternoon, doctors performed one last brain scan, but there was no change. David was not coming back. Although he was technically still alive, he was only being kept alive by machines. Doctors told Ellen that without the life-support machines, David would live for less than an hour.

With no show of emotion, Ellen plainly told doctors, "pull it," giving her consent to remove David's life-support. The doctors had never seen a parent with such detachment. Deanne noticed a slight smirk on Ellen's face that would haunt her for the rest of her life. Doctors pronounced David Boehm dead at 3:40 P.M. on November 26, 1988.

Ellen sat in a rocking chair in the hospital room, holding David's body just after his death. She rocked back and forth a few times and said, "Mommy loves you," but Deanne was troubled by the insincerity in her tone.

The medical examiner determined David had died of Sudden Infant Death Syndrome. SIDS, also known as "Crib Death," normally only occurred in infants less than one-year-old. David, however, was twenty-eight months. It was almost unheard of for a child of that age to die of SIDS.

The day after David's death, Ellen arranged for his funeral— then bought tickets for herself and Deanne for an upcoming wrestling match. Deanne suspected it was her odd way of coping with the loss.

Paul Boehm found out of his son's death not from Ellen, but from his mother-in-law. When he called Ellen, she complained that she couldn't afford a funeral for David. As a veteran, Paul suggested she use his veteran's benefits for a no-charge burial at Jefferson Barracks National Cemetery, but Ellen wouldn't hear of it. She wanted him to pay for a proper funeral.

David was buried at the Trinity Cemetery. Friends and co-workers in attendance said it was one of the saddest days they've ever experienced. Deanne was too distraught over the death and couldn't get herself to attend. Ellen, however, seemed cold and calm at the funeral, baffling others at her lack of emotion.

Paul was upset that Ellen had not buried David using his veteran's benefits, but he really had no say in the matter. He had only even seen his son once in his entire life.

Ellen's co-workers held a collection to raise money for her, knowing that she was working two jobs, got no support from Paul, and had to pay for the funeral herself.

Ellen held a $5,000 life insurance policy on each child provided by her employer. However, despite the $5,000 and another $1,000 raised by her co-workers, she refused to pay the $2,348 funeral bill. Instead, she bought a new car.

After David's death, Ellen's life returned to normal. She got regular manicures and continued attending wrestling matches. According to those around her, she almost seemed more upbeat than before.

One would think that having just lost a child, Ellen would be protective of her surviving children, but her actions showed exactly the opposite behavior. She enlisted her mother to watch her kids while she went on her wrestling trips, often not calling to check on them at all.

During August 1989, Ellen began calling insurance companies to get quotes for additional policies on Jennifer and Steven. She already had policies for $5,000 each from her employer, but she wanted more. She purchased several policies until each child was insured for $100,000. Ellen wasn't able to pay for her phone bill, which was inevitably disconnected, but she found the money for insurance policies, wrestling matches, and manicures.

September 13, 1989, was like any other day at the Boehm household. Ellen came home from work, cleaned the house, and made dinner. That night, after tucking Steven into bed and reading him a story, Jennifer brought her Barbie dolls into the bathroom to take a bath before going to bed.

Jennifer was unaware that her mother watched from the hallway while she washed herself and her dolls. As Jennifer rinsed her face and hair, Ellen plugged a hairdryer into the wall socket in the hallway and silently tossed it into Jennifer's bath water.

The electricity coursed through Jennifer's body as she frantically tried to get out of the tub. With her eyes closed, she had no idea what was going on or where the pain was coming from. She only knew she had to get out of the tub.

Jennifer's screams woke Steven, who ran toward the bathroom. When she saw Steven, Ellen unplugged the hairdryer and calmly asked her daughter, "How did the dryer get into the tub?"

A small bit of blood came out of the corner of Jennifer's mouth as she unsuccessfully tried to speak. Ellen told her to get dressed and they would go to the emergency room.

Both kids were screaming and Ellen went down the hall, to the apartment of a friend who was a medical student. He wasn't home. However, Jennifer and Stephen's screams had attracted the attention of neighbors, who called the police.

As Ellen and the kids stood outside of the building waiting for the police to arrive, Ellen made sure that the two of them had their story straight. Ellen told the children that Stephen had woken up, saw that Jennifer had washed the Barbie doll's hair and thought they would need to have their hair dried, so he plugged in the hairdryer and accidentally dropped it into the tub. Jennifer protested, knowing that it was a lie. Steven had been asleep when it happened and was nowhere near the bathroom.

Once at the emergency room, Jennifer reluctantly repeated the lie that it was all Steven's fault. After an examination, doctors noticed her pupils were dilated and she had petechial hemorrhages on her tongue, but otherwise she was okay and released.

Nine days later, Friday, September 9, was Steven's fourth birthday. The following day, Ellen brought him for a scheduled doctor visit to get his DTAP and Oral Polio vaccines. The doctor gave him a clean bill of health but said that the Pertussis vaccine may give him a mild fever and make him a little sick.

According to Ellen, Steven couldn't eat the rest of the day and vomited that evening. The following day, Sunday, she said he wasn't feeling much better, slept most of the day, and she fed him only liquids.

On Monday morning, Ellen planned to stay home from work to take care of Steven, claiming he was still feeling the side-effects of the vaccines. After sending Jennifer off to school, Ellen took Steven to her mother's house for a quick visit.

After leaving her mother's apartment, Ellen stopped by a payphone to call work. At 8:15 A.M. she told them she was taking Steven to the hospital, saying, "The same thing that happened to David is happening to Steven." But that was a lie.

As they drove toward their apartment, they passed the funeral home where David's funeral had been held. Steven told his mother, "I want to see David," and cried. She drove him to the cemetery so he could visit his brother's grave.

At 11:30 A.M., Ellen stopped at a payphone again to call her work. This time, she claimed they were going back to the hospital a second time. She told her employer that the first time they couldn't find anything wrong with him, but since then he had stopped breathing again.

After the call, Ellen drove Steven back to their apartment, where he sat in front of the television and watched Sesame Street while she cleaned the house.

That afternoon, Steven fell asleep in front of the television. Again, Ellen knelt on the floor next to her son, took the pillow from under his head, and smothered him.

Ellen ran out of her apartment and past the medical student's door. She went up the elevator to the eighth floor, to her friend Pauline's apartment, but she was on the wrong floor. Pauline lived on the sixth floor. Ellen then took the elevator back down to her own apartment and knocked on the door of Todd, the medical student, who immediately called 911.

Paramedics arrived at 12:59 P.M. to find Steven unresponsive on the floor. She told him he was watching television and suddenly stopped breathing. Paramedics rushed Steven to the hospital and, again, Ellen refused to ride in the ambulance, preferring to drive herself.

The ambulance arrived at the hospital at 1:24 P.M. but Ellen drove to her mother's house first and didn't arrive at the hospital until after 2:00 P.M.

From the hospital, Ellen called Deanne and left a message at her work saying,

> "The same thing that happened to David happened to Steven. He died sometime during the middle of the night."

At 4:00 P.M., Ellen called her work again to tell her co-workers that doctors were considering taking Steven off of life-support, but the truth was, Steven had been pronounced dead fifteen minutes earlier.

Ellen couldn't seem to keep her story straight and gave everyone she spoke to a slightly different version. Her stories got more convoluted when her co-workers came to the hospital to console her and she wasn't wearing her work clothes. She had specifically told them she had taken Steven to the hospital after she had dressed for work.

Ellen again seemed stoic at the death of her son. She spoke matter-of-factly about his death and that they had donated his eyes after his death.

Just minutes after her son's death, Ellen spoke to a friend in the hospital waiting room and noticed two young handsome men. As if she had completely forgotten what had just happened, Ellen pointed to the men and said,

> "I don't know what to do. Both of those men want to go out with me. They work at my office."

Deanne was confused and suspicious of Ellen's stories. She had been told that Steven died in the middle of the night, not that afternoon. Deanne was the first to notice that Ellen's stories made little sense and were a little too convenient. Nobody loses two children to SIDS, particularly not within a year of each other. Deanne called a friend that was a police sergeant and he put her in touch with a homicide detective.

————

Doctors tested Ellen and Jennifer for genetic cardiac issues and abnormal heart arrhythmia, but both checked out fine.

The medical examiner that examined Steven's body had ruled out all possible causes of death except for drugs, drowning, or mechanical asphyxia. When the toxicology report came back negative, the medical examiner sent his findings to seven respected medical experts for their opinions. Every expert ruled out any cause of death other than mechanical asphyxia.

After learning the cause of death, Police became concerned for Jennifer's safety and contacted Child Protective Services.

Child Protective Services questioned Jennifer and she initially gave Ellen's made-up version of the bathtub incident. Eventually, however, she broke down and told the truth. She admitted that her mother had instructed her to blame it on Steven. He was actually asleep when the hairdryer fell into the bathtub.

Investigators began talking to Ellen's friends, neighbors, and co-workers. Through various interviews, detectives learned of the additional life insurance purchases and the inconsistent stories from the day of Steven's death.

In early 1991, police had gathered enough evidence to arrest Ellen Boehm. FBI assisted local law enforcement in the arrest and she was pulled over as she drove home from work. In the interrogation room, detectives spread out reams of paper on the table and placed elaborate charts on the walls. The information all pertaining to her finances, insurance policies, and the children's medical records. Within minutes, Ellen confessed.

Displaying very little emotion or remorse, Ellen explained to detectives that she had been overwhelmed with debt, was getting no financial support from Paul, and felt she had no choice but to murder her children.

To avoid the death penalty, thirty-two-year-old Ellen Boehm pleaded guilty to one count of first-degree murder and one count of second-degree murder. She was sentenced to two life terms without the possibility of parole.

Custody of his surviving daughter, Jennifer, was not awarded to Paul Boehm. At eight years old, she was handed over to the Missouri Department of Social Services.

5

THE FAMILY MURDERS

The River Torrens flows from the peaks of Mount Pleasant, through the Adelaide Hills, to the Adelaide Plains and supplies water to the city center of Adelaide, Australia, before it continues into Gulf St. Vincent.

In the early 1970s, the area where the river flows through the base of the foothills was a popular "beat" for gay men to meet. Homosexuality was illegal at the time and South Australia's Vice Squad regularly patrolled the area.

In May 1972, corrupt police officers confronted three gay men, Roger James, Dr. George Duncan, and another man. Rather than cite the men for their crimes, the officers threw them in the rapid waters of River Torrens and left them to drown. Throwing gay men into the river was a common occurrence among the Vice Squad who considered it a "sport" and referred to the act as "flinging a poof."

Dr. George Duncan, a law lecturer at Adelaide University, drowned in the incident and was found 500 meters downstream. His death made him a martyr for gay rights activists in the area and the event helped repeal South Australia's anti-homosexuality laws.

The other two men were rescued that night with the help of a young man that was driving by. The young man was Bevan Spencer von Einem. von Einem drove the two men to the hospital and became a hero in Southern Australia. Although von Einem's first media appearance made him a hero, years later, he would return to the spotlight for much more sinister reasons.

———

Seven years later, sixteen-year-old Alan Barnes had spent the night at a friend's house in Adelaide. The following morning, a Sunday in June 1979, the teenager walked to Grand Junction Road to see if he could hitch a ride home. Hitchhiking had been common in the area at the time and was generally a safe way to get around the city. Although Alan was due home that Sunday afternoon, his parents allowed the boy his independence and didn't think too much of it when he hadn't returned home that day. When he hadn't arrived by Monday morning, however, Alan's mother knew something was wrong and called police.

Alan had long, blonde hair that stood out in a crowd. When police questioned people in the area, several remembered seeing him hitchhiking, but only one could provide any useful information. A motorist that had been driving on Grand Junction Road that morning claimed to have seen Alan getting into a car with three or four people. Unfortunately, the person was unable to give a description of the car or its passengers.

The following Sunday, just one week after Alan went missing, a couple hiking in the Adelaide Foothills near the South Para Reservoir came across an object along a trail beneath a bridge. As they approached, they could tell it was the body of a young male. The body had been twisted and contorted.

When police arrived, they found the body of a boy they believed to be in his twenties. It appeared someone had thrown the body over the railing of the bridge above, hoping it would land in the water. Instead, the body hit the dirt.

The news reports that evening announced that the body of a young man in his twenties was found deceased. When Alan's mother heard the news, she knew it had to be her son. She called police and said, "He's not in his twenties. He's sixteen. And if you look at the back of his watch, you'll see an engraving. It was his Christmas present."

It was indeed Alan. A postmortem examination of his body showed that he had died on Friday night or Saturday morning, just hours before he was dumped. Since he had been gone a week, that left the last six days of his life unaccounted for. His body had been meticulously washed clean in an attempt to hide evidence and he had been dressed in clothes that were not his own.

A toxicology examination revealed a large dose of a potent sedative called Noctec in his system. The condition of his body led police to believe that he had been drugged, severely beaten, brutally tortured, and held captive in the days before his death. Alan had died from massive blood loss in and around his anus. He had been raped with a large object, believed to be a bottle, which perforated the inside of his rectum. Clearly, it was the work of a psychotic sexual sadist.

———

Two months later, in August 1979, a man fishing from a dock at Mutton Cove, just Northwest of Adelaide, noticed a pair of black trash bags floating in the water along the bank of the Port Adelaide River. Curious, he opened one of the bags and called police when he saw what looked like butchered human remains inside.

The bags had been placed in the water just a mile from where the river flowed into the ocean. The killer assumed the current would carry the bags into the open sea, but they had caught on a dock.

When detectives opened the bag, it was enough to bring seasoned officers to tears. The first bag contained a male torso with the chest cavity cut open. The organs had been removed from the torso and placed into smaller plastic bags. The severed legs and arms had been stripped of skin and muscle tissue and placed into the chest cavity. The head had been severed from the body and strangely wired to the chest.

A medical examination determined the victim died in a similar manner to Alan Barnes. He had been tortured and bled to death from anal injuries. He had been brutally raped with a bottle-shaped object which had perforated his rectum and anus. There was evidence of blunt force trauma to his head, but not enough to have caused death.

Alan Barnes / Neil Muir

The body was identified as Neil Muir, a twenty-five-year-old gay heroin user that was well known to police. Neil lived alone and had only been reported missing two days before the body was found. Detectives weren't quite sure how long he had been missing. Like Alan Barnes, Neil had been last seen on a Sunday. Both bodies had been discarded in or near water and both had died of blood loss from anal injuries. Though the similarities seem glaringly obvious in hindsight, the two murders weren't initially linked together.

———

Shortly after the body of Neil Muir was discovered, police received an anonymous phone call from someone that referred to himself as "Mr. B." The caller told detectives he believed that Bevan Spencer von Einem was responsible for the murders. von Einem's name was added to a list of leads, along with hundreds of others.

When detectives interviewed von Einem, he freely admitted that he knew Neil Muir. The two of them had been lovers four years earlier. von Einem claimed to have met with Neil a few days before he went missing, but hadn't seen him since. Although it was a significant finding, the information was lost in the hundreds of other leads detectives needed to follow up on.

————

Two years had gone by with very little development in either murder. On February 27, 1982, nineteen-year-old Mark Langley attended a friend's birthday party. After the party, he and two friends went for a drive through the city. As they drove near the River Torrens, Mark had an argument with his friends, got out of the car, and told them he would walk home. Mark's friends drove off, but it had been a petty argument and, just minutes later, his friends had a change of heart. They turned around to pick him up, but Mark was nowhere to be found. Assuming he had found a ride home, they went home without him.

The following morning, Mark's father called the police to report him missing. Mark's friends and family searched the area where he was last seen, but he had simply vanished. Divers were sent to search the River Torrens but found nothing. Nine days after Mark went missing, his body was found in an area called Summertown at the base of Mount Lofty, just east of Adelaide.

Unlike the other victims, Mark's body had no visible external injuries. His clothes were clean, but his blue undershirt was missing, as was his silver necklace with a zodiac pendant. He died, however, just like the others—from massive blood loss due to injuries to his anus and rectum caused by the insertion of a bottle-shaped object. Also, similar to Alan Barnes, Mark's body had been washed clean before it was dumped.

Strangely, Mark's body had a small, recent, vertical surgical scar. Someone had performed surgery on him just below his navel, even taking the time to shave him before surgery. The wound was stitched closed with surgical thread and Johnson & Johnson surgical tape afterwards. Medical examiners and investigators believed the surgery was performed in order to retrieve an object that may have been caught in his intestines - possibly an object that the killer believed could have contained a fingerprint.

Like the victims before, Mark had been given alcohol and a massive amount of a sedative called Mandrax, more widely known as methaqualone or quaalude.

Detectives finally began to consider the possibility that the three murders were linked. As a result, they began looking into other missing person cases that may also have been related. That's when they noticed the case file of Peter Stogneff.

———

On August 27, 1981, exactly six months before Mark Langley's disappearance, fourteen-year-old Peter Stogneff made plans with a friend to skip school. Before he left home that morning, he dropped his school backpack in his garage and took the bus into the city to meet his friend. Peter's friend waited patiently at the local shopping mall, but Peter never showed. Later that evening, when Peter didn't return home, his parents called the police to report him missing. An extensive search ensued, but Peter had vanished without a trace. The only clue was a witness at

Tea Tree Plaza that claimed they saw the boy with an adult male.

Almost a year later in a small town just north of Adelaide, a farmer conducting a burn-off (a fire-management process used to encourage plant growth and reduce wildfires) discovered a human skeleton in the ashes. Unfortunately, any evidence that may have been at the scene was now charred. Using dental records, investigators determined it was the remains of Peter Stogneff. Although they were unable to determine an official cause of death, medical examiners could tell that the spine had been severed with a saw and his legs had been sawed just above the knees.

———

For the next fifteen months, the cases went nowhere. Police briefly thought they had found the killer: Dr. Peter Millhouse, a doctor who had known Neil Muir. Prosecutors brought a case against the man based on weak circumstantial evidence, but at trial he was easily acquitted. They were back to square one.

———

On a Sunday afternoon in July 1983, fifteen-year-old Richard Kelvin and his friend Boris were at a local park kicking around a soccer ball. Richard was a handsome, athletic boy with a steady girlfriend and got good grades in school. That afternoon, as a joke, he wore the family dog's collar around his neck as he played with Boris in the park.

Peter Stogneff / Richard Kelvin

When it was time to go home, the two boys walked to the bus stop and Richard waited as Boris caught his bus home. Richard began his walk home, less than a quarter of a mile from the bus stop, but he never made it. He had simply disappeared.

The case of Richard Kelvin's disappearance drew more attention in the media than the other cases. Richard was the son of a well-known local newscaster that worked for Channel 9. Richard had been wearing a Channel 9 t-shirt when he disappeared.

Initially, local police assumed Richard had simply run away from home. His frustrated parents protested and explained that Richard was a good kid; he would never run away from home. Police had wasted two days and Richard still hadn't returned home. That Tuesday, police finally began a door-to-door search of the area and came up with a clue.

A man living nearby that worked as a security guard told police that on the Sunday evening when Richard went missing, he heard shouting on the street near his home. He said he could hear arguing, cries for help, and car doors slamming on the street nearby. One voice sounded young, several others were adults, and one voice appeared to be that of a woman. Immediately after the argument, he heard the loud exhaust of a car speeding away. By the time he looked outside, the car was gone. Other neighbors in the area corroborated the same story. It appeared as though a group of people had abducted Richard.

The location from which Richard was abducted was just a few blocks from where Mark Langley was last seen. Police and media immediately suspected that Richard may have been abducted by the same killer or killers as the other four victims. Theories arose that he possibly was abducted by sexual deviants because of the dog collar he wore around his neck.

Because of Richard's high-profile father, the story became front-page news. Everyone in the area seemed to have theories about what had happened and the police were inundated with calls. Anonymous callers told police he was being held in a camper near the mountains while others claimed to have seen his death in a snuff film.

Finally, seven weeks after Richard vanished, a family walking through the forest near Mount Crawford, northeast of Adelaide, came across what they thought was someone lying in the bushes in a fetal position. The father assumed it may be a man that was injured, but it soon became obvious that it was a dead body. As soon as the man noticed his Channel 9 shirt and the dog collar, he knew it was the body of Richard Kelvin.

An autopsy revealed exactly the same cause of death as the others: massive blood loss from anal injuries. His body had been washed clean and redressed in his own clothes. Richard, however, had been missing for much longer than the others. The state of decomposition revealed that he had been dead for only a week in the scrub brush. That meant that Richard had endured five to six weeks of excruciating torture and sexual abuse before his death.

Like the others, Richard's body contained a massive cocktail of powerful sedatives including Noctec (Chloral Hydrate), Mandrax (Quaalude), Valium (Diazepam), Rohypnol (roofies), and Amobarbital. It was clear to detectives that all five deaths were linked.

———

Six months prior to Richard Kelvin's murder, a young man named George informed police he had been kidnapped, drugged, and raped by several people. He told detectives that while hitchhiking, he was picked up by an older man who offered him alcohol in the backseat of his car and enticed him to come to a nearby house to drink with some older women. At the house, the women flirted with him and gave him more alcohol. After some time, he began feeling drowsy and the last thing he remembered was being taken into a bedroom to have sex with one of the women. Just before he blacked out, he realized that the woman was not female, but a transvestite.

George woke up the next day in his own home, but crippled with pain and no recollection of the rest of the night or how he got home. He went to the police to report the incident and agreed to a medical and toxicological test. He had severe lacerations in his anus and his blood contained a significant quantity of Mandrax. It was the same drug that was found in the systems of Richard Kelvin and Mark Langley.

Detectives searched through prior police reports and found many similar stories. There were several other young men that had also been abducted, drugged, and raped.

Mandrax had become a popular recreational drug in the late 1970s, known on the street as "Randy Mandys." It was a date-rape drug. This led the South Australia government to regulate it and several other drugs. After its regulation, every prescription of the drug had a paper trail and police believed their best option was to search for who had access to these drugs.

Detectives took the time to sift through thousands of records of individuals in South Australia that had been prescribed Mandrax. After extensive searches, the name Bevan Spencer von Einem came up.

———

Bevan Spencer von Einem

At first appearance, von Einem seemed normal enough. He was in his late thirties, prematurely gray, worked as an accountant, and still lived with his mother. Detectives questioned von Einem at his workplace and at home without prior notice. They wanted to surprise him and not give him the opportunity to prepare his answers. When asked about his prescriptions, von Einem explained he was an insomniac and had trouble sleeping his entire life. He claimed the prescriptions for Mandrax and Rohypnol were to help him sleep. He flatly denied knowing any of the victims other than Neil Muir.

When asked about his whereabouts on the night Richard Kelvin was kidnapped, he had an answer prepared. He claimed he was home sick with the flu the entire week and his mother could back up his story.

von Einem seemed to have prepared answers for every question, often giving racist comments baselessly suggesting that people like Lebanese, Greek, or Italian immigrants must have committed the murders. When asked point-blank if he had committed the murders, he gave a strange response, telling the detectives,

"No, of course not. That would be unethical."

———

Detectives tracked down the anonymous caller, "Mr. B," who had mentioned von Einem years earlier. He agreed to speak to detectives again on the condition that he could remain anonymous. Mr. B was in his early twenties, which meant he would have been a teenager when he associated with von Einem. He claimed he would ride with von Einem while he drove around Adelaide, picking up young boys on the streets.

The men would offer boys a ride and give them alcohol from a cooler that von Einem always kept in the back seat of his car. After a few drinks, the boys were invited to a party with more alcohol and women. von Einem would then offer the boys what he told them was "NoDoz", a popular caffeine pill at the time. But rather than caffeine, the pills were actually one of his powerful sedatives.

After the boys had passed out from the sedatives, Mr. B claimed von Einem would take the boys to a house owned by two transgender women, where they would be raped by multiple men, often with a bottle. Afterwards, most of them would be released with only a vague recollection of what had happened to them.

Mr. B's explanation was virtually the same as what the young man, George, had told them. Although police were glad to have the information about von Einem, they believed that Mr. B had more involvement than he was admitting. The young man had been careful not to implicate himself, however, and claimed to have witnessed the events, but never participated.

————

In the Fall of 1983, investigators searched von Einem's home he shared with his mother. Although there was no evidence of a murder having happened at the residence, they did find his prescription for Mandrax in his bathroom. He claimed that was the only drug he had, but when police continued their search, several more drugs were found in a duffel bag. Even more were hidden on a secret ledge hidden behind his closet. The drugs were the same that had been found in the bodies of the victims: Noctec, Valium, and Rohypnol. Samples were also taken of von Einem's hair and blood.

On the evening after the search of von Einem's home, detectives parked nearby and watched as a man who would later become known as "Mr. R" visited von Einem. Mr. R was a businessman in Adelaide and a close friend of von Einem. The man remained at the house for several hours.

————

Bevan Spencer von Einem was arrested and charged with the murder of Richard Kelvin on November 3, 1983. Prosecutors believed the link between the drugs found in Richard Kelvin's body and the drugs found in von Einem's home was enough to convict him for that murder. The other four murders would have to wait.

Over the next several months, detectives gathered evidence. Of the 925 fibers found on Richard Kelvin's clothing, 250 of them came from von Einem's bedroom carpet, bedspread, and cardigan sweater. von Einem's hairs were found inside Richard's jeans.

Between December 1978 and August 1983, von Einem had been prescribed 5,873 tablets and capsules of the six different types of sedatives, often filling the prescriptions from three different pharmacists on the same day.

————

Police believed that von Einem murdered all five boys, but he wasn't alone. He had to have had help. Neil Muir had been butchered in such a way that they believed someone with surgery experience was involved. The same experience would have been needed for the surgery that was done to Mark Langley. There were accounts of several people in a car abducting Richard Kelvin, while additional accounts pointed toward several other men involved in the rapes, as well as transgender women.

Investigators searched a building owned by von Einem's associate, Mr. R, in central Adelaide. The entire second floor of the building was vacant, with only a mattress lying on the floor. Police believed this could have been a location they used to rape the young boys.

Mr. R was a gay man that was known to spend his lunch breaks cruising gay areas of Adelaide looking for young men. His roommate was a doctor named Stephen George Woodwards. Woodwards had been accused multiple times of sexual assault, eventually facing charges. Police believed Woodwards could have performed the surgery that was done to Mark Langley.

Although detectives were able to show that von Einem ran in the same circles as these men, they had trouble directly linking them to any of the crimes.

———

With the discovery of the fibers and hairs on Richard Kelvin's clothes, von Einem changed his story. Initially, he had claimed he was sick with the flu for a full week during Richard's disappearance. He even had a prescription filled. Now he claimed he had been driving in the area to get some fish and chips when he encountered Richard Kelvin. He told detectives he struck up a conversation with Richard and the fifteen-year-old boy came with him willingly. He claimed they drove around the city and talked. Richard spoke to him at length about school problems and girlfriend problems. von Einem claimed he then brought Richard back to his home, where they talked some more. He said that at one point he put his arm around Richard, which he explained as the reason that fibers from his cardigan were found on Richard's clothes. He claimed that the carpet fibers on Richard's body were from when he sat on the floor while von Einem played the harp for him. von Einem then explained that he gave Richard $20 for a taxi ride back home and that was the last he had seen of him.

Detectives didn't buy his story for a minute. The fibers from von Einem's carpet and his own hairs were found on the inside of Richard's clothing, not the outside. Also, Richard had died five weeks after he went missing. Any such fibers from the day he went missing would have been gone by that amount of time.

More importantly, von Einem had just admitted that he was the last person to see Richard alive. Despite the evidence against him, von Einem pleaded not-guilty.

Bevan Spencer von Einem's trial started on October 15, 1984. His defense tried to imply that Richard Kelvin was secretly bisexual, which wasn't true, and ultimately didn't make a difference to their case. von Einem was found guilty on November 5 after less than eight hours of deliberation. The conviction came with an automatic life sentence with parole eligibility in twenty-four years. Eight of those years could be taken off for good behavior.

von Einem could conceivably have been released in as little as sixteen years. The Attorney General, however, filed an immediate appeal to lengthen the parole period. As a result, his parole eligibility was extended to thirty-six years.

The first guest to visit von Einem in jail was Mr. R

———

In the years after von Einem's conviction, detectives searched for evidence to convict von Einem or any accomplices for the additional four murders. A $250,000 reward was offered for information leading to an arrest and over time the reward was gradually increased to $1,000,000, but with no results.

Mr. B continued to provide the prosecution with information claiming that von Einem and Mr. R had made a snuff film of the killing of Alan Barnes. He also told police that von Einem had been involved in the Beaumont Children's disappearance in 1966, as well as the disappearance of two girls from an Australian rules football match in 1973. Of course, the accusations were just Mr. B's word without actual evidence.

Mr. B's sister contacted police and claimed that her brother once told her he had participated in the abduction and murder of a young man in Adelaide. She claimed they threw the body off a bridge. Again, without actual evidence.

By 1990, armed only with circumstantial evidence, prosecutors brought von Einem back to trial for the murders of Alan Barnes and Mark Langley. In a massive blow to the prosecution, much of the evidence presented, however, was deemed inadmissible by the court. In order to avoid a possible acquittal, the charges were eventually dropped.

———

One of the detectives working the case appeared on the television news show "60 Minutes." During the show, he spoke of his desire to break up "the happy family," referring to his belief that there were many more people helping von Einem commit the crimes. He believed there was evidence linking wealthy Adelaide businessmen, politicians, judges, and doctors, all child sex abusers.

Over the next few decades, the case remained the subject of conspiracy theories throughout South Australia. Many people believed to have been involved remain with their identity hidden, while others have been revealed.

———

Mr. R - Known to be a longtime friend of von Einem and visited him in prison multiple times. Police have long suspected him as an accomplice to the murders but were unable to produce evidence.

Dr. Stephen Woodwards - Woodwards refused to answer questions to police. Investigators believed he supplied von Einem with drugs and may have helped butcher the victims, as well as sexually assaulting them.

Denis St Denis - Another of von Einem's longtime friends as well as his hairdresser. Police believe Richard Kelvin was held at St Denis' home while he was tortured and killed.

Mr. B - Although he was careful not to implicate himself when questioned by police, detectives believe he was involved in many of the abductions.

Prudence Firman - A transgender woman who had a sex change in 1982 is believed to have allowed use of her home for abductions in exchange for drugs.

Noel Terrance Brooks - Was believed to have been seen with Peter Stogneff on the day he disappeared.

Derrance Stevenson - A high profile lawyer that was an associate of Alan Barnes. Stevenson dealt heroin from his home and was known for his predilection for young boys. He was murdered by his nineteen-year-old lover, David Szach, just weeks after Alan's murder.

Gino Gambardella - Fled Australia to Italy after several accusations of sexual assault. He's a close friend of both von Einem and Stevenson.

The list of suspected involved parties goes on and on.

Another gay man with an association to von Einem was Trevor Peters. After his death in 2014, his family found a diary as they sifted through his belongings.

Entries in the diary discussed his relationship with von Einem in detail and several others listed above. The diary alleged that von Einem had discussed the abduction of Alan Barnes with his hairdresser, Denis St Denis, and laughed about taking photos of Barnes as he was being held captive.

Lewis Turtur

Another person implicated in the diary was Lewis Turtur. Turtur was well-known as a flamboyant drag queen whose brother was a famous Olympic athlete. When news crews confronted Turtur about his association with von Einem, Turtur admitted his involvement and admitted to abducting boys, but insisted he had nothing to do with the murders.

> "All I know is they came in... he dropped them off at our place, he went home, we let them sleep it off, they left in the morning. I was a stupid fool, wasn't I? Half the time I was drugged out anyway, so I don't really care. I was in my own little world."

Investigators believe there may have been as many as 150 abductions and many more murders throughout the years that have been unreported or unlinked. Although many associates of von Einem, all with a passion for young boys, were believed to have been involved, none have ever been charged.

6

THE EGYPTIAN BEAUTY

Bill Nelson liked to stand out in a crowd. He was a large man who wore red cowboy boots, a huge shiny gold belt buckle, and loved driving his bright-red Corvette. Originally from Texas, he had five children with seventeen grandchildren and claimed to have once owned a cattle ranch.

During the 1980s, Bill had been a pilot in Laredo, Texas, where he flew DC-3 propeller planes back and forth across the border of Mexico. On one of his trips back to Laredo, he was arrested after landing the plane full of marijuana. It was rumored that Bill had worked with the CIA at one time, but that didn't help his case. He was convicted on the smuggling charge and spent four years in a federal prison.

In October 1991, Bill was fifty-six-years-old and settling his life down in Costa Mesa, California. He often drank cheap beer and played pool at a local dive bar. That's where he met twenty-three-year-old Omaima Aref. Omaima was a petite Egyptian beauty and a pretty good pool player. With her exotic good looks, dark skin, and long curly hair, she too stood out in a crowd. Despite the thirty-three-year age difference, Bill took an instant liking to her. That night, after several games of pool, Bill and Omaima started their whirlwind romance.

———

Early life had not been easy for Omaima. She was born in a poor Egyptian farming village near the border of Sudan. According to Omaima, her father was a violent man that regularly abused her both physically and sexually. When her parents divorced, she and her mother moved to a village in Cairo known as The City of the Dead, a centuries-old slum made up of thousands of graves, tombs, and mausoleums. Many inhabitants of the city lived in the tombs alongside the dead.

When she was seventeen, Omaima met an American man that had been working in Cairo as an oil worker. Muslim men weren't interested in her because it was known that she wasn't a virgin, so Omaima knew the American would be her ticket out of the slums of Cairo. Omaima married the American man and when his job ended in Cairo, they returned to his home state of Texas. But soon after her arrival in the United States, their relationship fell apart and they divorced. At just eighteen, Omaima found herself alone with no real skills to speak of and a poor grasp of the English language.

Omaima made her way to California, where her exotic looks got her occasional work as a model. When she couldn't find modeling work, she took jobs as a nanny. But rather than work, Omaima found it much easier to meet men in bars with hopes that she could find a man to take care of her. If that didn't work, she just stole from them, often tying them to their bed and stealing their money or vehicles.

———

When Omaima met Bill Nelson, she immediately saw a potential meal-ticket. Bill ran his own business refurbishing computers in his home. Though his accommodations were humble, he otherwise gave off an aura of wealth.

Within weeks of their meeting, Bill and Omaima were like teenage lovers and he asked her to drive across the country with him, to Texas and Arkansas, to meet his family. But when they drove east on Interstate 10, they only got as far as Phoenix before Bill asked her to marry him. After knowing each other for less than a month, they drove into downtown Phoenix and got married by a Justice of the Peace.

Omaima poses on Bill Nelson's red Corvette - Bill and Omaima on their trip to Texas

When Bill and Omaima arrived in Texas, his family was stunned. She didn't fit his personality at all – not to mention she was younger than some of his own children. Although they didn't necessarily agree with his decision to marry her, his family saw that they were happy together. The two enjoyed their time with his family and continued their cross-country drive back to Costa Mesa.

―――――

In the late afternoon of Thanksgiving Day 1991, Bill called his step-daughter to wish her a happy Thanksgiving. They discussed the dinner they had earlier in the day and their plans for the long weekend. That was to be the last time anyone spoke to Bill Nelson.

―――――

José Esquivel was enjoying his Sunday morning by sleeping in late on December 1, 1991. Just after 9:00 A.M., he heard a loud pounding on his front door. Startled, he looked out his bedroom window to see a bright red Corvette in his drive-way. It was a car that he didn't recognize. Assuming someone had the wrong house, he ignored the knocking and went back to sleep.

Four hours later, the frantic pounding started again at the front door. When José answered the door, he saw a disheveled Omaima Nelson. He had dated her briefly a year earlier, but hadn't heard from her since.

Omaima was covered with bruises, small cuts, and what seemed to be spots of dried blood. She frantically told him she needed his help. She explained that her husband, of only a few weeks, raped her and beat her. But what she asked next shook him to his core. She said she had killed him, cut up his body, and needed help to dispose of the trash bags that held his body parts.

José was speechless. He barely knew this woman and she wanted him to help get rid of a body. Omaima went on to explain that on Thanksgiving evening, he had tied her up and raped her. She said that when she managed to free herself; she took the lamp from the nightstand and hit him over the head. Then she stabbed him with scissors. He was dead and she panicked. She spent the next two days cutting him up and putting the pieces of him into black plastic trash bags. Omaima told José that Bill had $75,000 in cash in his safe.

> "If you help me get rid of the body, you can have the money and his two motorcycles."

José kept calm and played along. He told Omaima to wait there at his house while he left to go get his truck. He said he would return in 30 minutes. She waited nervously at his house when the police knocked on the door. José had driven to the nearest payphone and told police everything that Omaima had said.

When police questioned Omaima, she was clearly distraught and still crying. At first glance, her visible injuries on her face and arms seemed to back up her story of sexual assault. She completely denied telling José that she had killed her husband or offered him money to help dispose of the body. She told the officers that her husband was just away on a business trip to Florida and very much alive.

Police still found her story suspicious and examined the red Corvette in the driveway. From the passenger side window, they could see a black plastic bag on the front seat. When they opened the door and reached into the bag, they were shocked to find it filled with blood smeared newspapers and what appeared to be human organs.

When Omaima was brought into the police station for questioning, she again firmly denied telling José anything about killing her husband. She paced back and forth in the interview room for nearly four hours as detectives interrogated her. When asked about the bag of organs in the car, she blamed it on Bill. She told detectives of Bill's past criminal record and said she believed her husband may have killed someone. She claimed Bill had raped her and raped other women. Omaima rambled on about hallucinations and spoke of herself in the third person.

After the interview, Omaima was taken to the hospital for a sexual assault examination. However, doctors noticed that the cuts and bruises on her arms, breast, and head were not defensive wounds. Moreover, a rape test showed no evidence of vaginal or anal trauma.

Investigators then searched the apartment she shared with Bill Nelson. To say the home was messy would be an understatement. Boxes, computer parts, and miscellaneous junk covered every inch of the apartment. But apart from being horrible housekeepers, at first glance it didn't seem that there were signs of a struggle. When the forensic team looked a little closer, however, they found a much more gruesome scene.

It started with a drop of blood on a doorknob. Then a small pool of blood on the carpet. When they worked their way into the kitchen, they were in for a shock. What appeared to be parts of the Thanksgiving turkey in a deep fryer were actually human hands cooked in oil. The garbage can contained parts of a human hip with turkey and cranberry sauce. Wrapped in foil in the freezer, tucked behind frozen vegetables, was Bill Nelson's severed head. It, too, had been cooked to a crisp.

When investigators pulled the sheets off of the bed, they found the mattress soaked with so much blood that it bled through to the box springs. Ultimately, when they weighed the remains of Bill Nelson that they found in the house, more than one hundred pounds were missing compared to the weight listed on his driver's license. The downstairs neighbor in the apartment building told police he had heard the garbage disposal running for hours all weekend long. She systematically carved him up and shoved him down the kitchen drain.

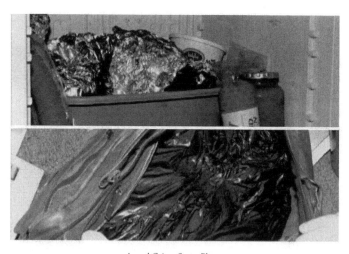

Actual Crime Scene Photos

Scattered throughout the house were more and more body parts stuffed into black plastic trash bags. Investigators also found a trash bag containing a broken bedside lamp and a clothes iron, both covered in blood.

In the bedroom, there appeared to be evidence that supported Omaima's claim of sexual assault. There was rope laying on the bedroom floor and the bedposts had been broken. However, when investigators examined what was left of Bill Nelson's ankles, the ligature marks revealed *he* was the one that had been tied up, not Omaima.

———

When Omaima was brought back into the interrogation room, she confessed to killing her husband. She claimed, however, that she had no recollection of it at all.

> "I don't remember how I killed him. All I remember… I get up, like I said, and find him and he's in a trash bag. I wish I knew how I killed him, though."

> "Something inside me told me that I had to do it. Like demons."

Again, Omaima rambled at length about taking drugs and alcohol. She gave cryptic answers in a feeble attempt to seem mentally ill. She told detectives she had hallucinated and had been contacted and instructed by mysterious spirits.

> "Two women. There was blood all over them. And they walk in and said 'He must die. He must die.'"

The medical examiner determined Bill Nelson died of over twenty-five blows to the head, most likely with the bedside lamp and the clothes iron. She then repeatedly stabbed him with a pair of scissors. The coroner's office commented that the body had been dismembered with such precision that they wondered if Omaima had cut up a body before. The cuts seemed to have been done by someone with experience.

———

When police looked into Omaima's prior arrest record, they found a long list of offenses. Several times she had met men in bars, lured them in with the prospect of kinky sex, tied them up, and stolen their money. She had also stolen a man's car. She had been arrested for petty theft and shoplifting as well. On one occasion, when two department store security guards suspected her of shoplifting, she bit the female security guard in the breast, almost severing her breast. She grabbed the other guard in the crotch, bringing him to his knees. Omaima ran, but was eventually apprehended and arrested for shoplifting and battery, spending two months in jail for the altercation.

When news of the murder and how she had lured Bill Nelson to his death hit the media, a man came forward with additional information for detectives. Robert Hansson told detectives that Omaima had lived with him briefly just one year before she met Bill Nelson. He said their relationship was based entirely on sex. When she told him she wanted money, he asked what she was going to do for him. Her reply was, "I want to tie you up." Hansson thought, "Okay, this sounds kinda kinky," and agreed. Once he was tied to the bedposts, she pulled out a handgun and demanded money. Hansson was able to break himself free, took the gun away from her, and kicked her out of his house. He told police he was embarrassed about the incident and hadn't reported it to police.

―――――

The trial of twenty-four-year-old Omaima Nelson began on December 2, 1992. Her attorney argued that she had been beaten and abused by Bill Nelson since the beginning of their short marriage. She blamed her actions on a history of abuse dating back to her childhood. According to Omaima, everyone in her family had either beaten, tortured, or molested her.

During the trial it was revealed that at seven-years-old Omaima was subjected to genital mutilation, also known as female circumcision. It was a dangerous ritual common in many countries where the external female genitalia are removed without anesthesia or sterilized surgical instruments. The practice is an attempt to control a woman's sexuality and results in very painful intercourse. The procedure left her with scar tissue and sensitivity in the area that made enjoyment of sex impossible.

Omaima claimed Bill demanded sex from her on a daily basis and often complained that she wasn't performing to his expectations. As a result of his sexual assaults, she castrated him and disposed of his genitals using the garbage disposal.

The defense argued that her history of abuse caused deep emotional scars for her that led her to butcher her husband when he sexually assaulted her. A forensic psychologist presented by the defense testified that Omaima was a deeply disturbed woman who believed she was descended from ancient Egyptians. These ancient Egyptians spoke and acted through her when she killed Bill Nelson.

Omaima Nelson at trial and years later in prison

The forensic psychologist also testified that Omaima had told her she cooked Bill Nelson's ribs in the oven, slathered them with barbecue sauce, and ate them. She claimed,

"they tasted sweet, just like I like it."

Omaima later, however, denied that she ate any part of her husband.

To explain why she dismembered him, her defense explained that the Egyptians believed that if a body were scattered, it couldn't ascend to the afterlife. She wanted to make sure that, if she made it to the afterlife, he wouldn't be there too.

The Prosecution, however, argued that an examination of Omaima's body proved there was no evidence of rape and the ligature marks on Bill's body showed that he was the one restrained, not her. Prosecutors also shrugged off the defense's explanation of her psychiatric issues. The story of the ancient Egyptians was all just theatrics to develop an insanity plea.

On the witness stand, Omaima told the court that Bill had threatened to kill her on the drive to Texas. She claimed that if she didn't do as she was told, he would bury her body in the desert. Photos and video of their cross-country drive, however, showed them both happy and carefree.

———

On January 12, 1993, Omaima Nelson was found guilty of murdering her husband of less than a month. However, without proof of premeditation, the jury couldn't reach a unanimous decision of first-degree murder. She was instead convicted of a lesser charge of second-degree murder. She was also convicted of the attempted robbery of Robert Hansson and sentenced to twenty-seven years to life in prison.

During her incarceration, Omaima met and married a man in his seventies. He came to the prison in his wheelchair for three-day conjugal visits until he died and left her his estate. During his visits, they stayed together in accommodations equipped with kitchen knives and he reportedly had no fear of her.

In 2006 she was denied parole when

"commissioners found her unpredictable and a serious threat to public safety."

She was denied parole a second time in 2011 when the parole board determined "she had not taken responsibility for the murder, and would not be a productive citizen if she were freed."

7

HER DISSOCIATIVE STATE

Betty Devore was born and raised in Jefferson County, Iowa, a tiny rectangular spot of land near the southeastern corner of the state. From the 1920s until 2000, the population of the entire county barely reached over 16,000.

Small town life wasn't easy for Betty. Her mother had been in and out of mental institutions ever since she could remember. She and her siblings suffered physical and mental abuse at the hands of both her father and mother. On one occasion, her mother had thrown a butcher's knife at her.

When Betty was nine years old, she and her sister were raped in a barn by a man that had worked with their father. When the man was finished with the two young girls, he held up a large ball-peen hammer and threatened that if either of them ever said a word about the rape, he would smash both of their heads to a bloody pulp. Young Betty tucked the memory in the back of her mind and did her best to forget it ever happened.

In her early teenage years, Betty's mother had a nervous breakdown and was hospitalized. Her treatment for depression included eighty-two electric shock treatments. During her hospitalization, Betty witnessed her father having sex with a girlfriend that he had on the side, adding to Betty's trauma.

When Betty was old enough to leave home, however, she met Dale Guffey and the two were married. For a brief time after the birth of their second son in 1969, Betty was admitted to a mental hospital as well. Dale later recalled that Betty just hadn't been herself: "She was someplace else." She would scream about random things, but he never quite knew why she was upset.

During Betty and Dale's eighteen year marriage, they had four children. Except for the hospitalization, the marriage was good. There was never any physical abuse by either of them, but the marriage had simply run its course and they divorced in the late 1980s. Their older boys stayed with their father, while their eleven-year-old daughter, Heather, chose to live with Betty.

————

In late February 1988, Betty found herself single again and read a notice in the local paper about a meeting for singles in Fairfield. With a population of just under 10,000, Fairfield, Iowa, was the largest city in the county. When she met fifty-six-year-old Harold Frieberg, the large man towered at least a foot over her small frame. Harold, too, was recently single. He was a natural charmer, owned a farm in nearby Libertyville, and ran a business selling antique furniture from his home.

Betty Frieberg

Betty and Harold hit it off immediately and started dating. He swept her off her feet. After only three weeks of dating, they were married and Betty and Heather moved into his farmhouse. It was Harold's fifth marriage. Each of the prior four marriages had ended in divorce and resulted in six children that all lived with their mothers.

Betty worked for Banker's Life and Casualty Insurance selling life insurance from their home. Although she and Heather had no experience with farming, they also helped with the farm and Harold's antique business. During the first year of living on the farm, Harold and his new step-daughter got along well, so it wasn't long before he adopted her as his own.

Although Harold had six children from prior marriages, he had almost no contact with any of them. He incessantly complained that the ex-wives all wanted his money and he didn't believe that any of the children loved him, nor even wanted anything to do with him. It was Harold that suggested to Betty that he buy life insurance from her. In 1989, Betty sold him three life insurance policies totaling $250,000 and Betty was listed as the beneficiary of each.

Betty recalled that the first two years of marriage were wonderful. Her relationship with Harold was loving – until something suddenly changed during the winter of 1990. There was a sudden snap. Whatever had attracted Harold to Betty was abruptly gone. From that point on there was a steady pattern of abuse that brought Betty back to memories of her childhood.

Two of Harold's ex-wives were suing him for back alimony and child support that he had refused to pay over the past ten years. Later, one of the bulls had died, causing problems on the farm. Everything that went wrong in Harold's life became misdirected anger toward Betty.

That winter the farm house had settled, causing a crack in one of the interior walls. For some reason Harold saw that as Betty's fault. He kicked her foot while wearing his work boots, fracturing her toe and requiring a trip to the hospital.

From that point forward, he screamed and berated her in every possible scenario. The house wasn't clean, the meals weren't cooked to his liking, or the work on the farm wasn't done correctly. Each time Betty was yelled at. Eventually, the yelling was accompanied by backhanded slaps across her face, or he would grab her arms and shake her violently.

Everything that happened suddenly became Betty's fault. Or Heather's. The daughter that he so proudly adopted just a year before was also a target of his abuse. He would call the fourteen-year-old "stupid" for minor mistakes, like putting the wrong price tag on antique furniture or doing her chores incorrectly. She, too, endured slaps, whippings with his leather belt, and having her hair pulled. On her fourteenth birthday, she lied to her friends to explain away the bruising and scratches on her face.

In another instance, he stripped off Betty's clothes and rubbed foot powder inside her vagina, yelling,

"Maybe you can lose some weight from the inside!"

Heather had witnessed the abuse of her mother on several occasions by her adoptive father. He had suddenly turned into a violent monster. As the months passed, the abuse escalated. Heather watched as he strangled Betty with an alarm clock cord he had ripped from the wall. On another occasion, Heather witnessed her father throwing a five-gallon bucket, hitting Betty in the back of the head. When Betty hadn't cooked a meal to his liking, he stabbed her in the arm. Every day came with the constant threat of violence for Betty and Heather.

The abuse seemed endless. Harold showed dominance over his wife by placing the cords of an electric fence charger on each side of her head and neck, shocking her for three to four minutes.

Betty was unsure how much more she could take. If he continued at this rate, someday he'd kill her. Or Heather. One day while Betty was working on the farm, he kicked her in the chest, knocking her off of a combine and into the field. He then chased her through the field screaming,

"I'm going to chop you into little pieces."

The fall had injured her leg, requiring medical treatment and time in a wheelchair.

It became an everyday occurrence for Harold to demean his wife with insults about her weight, calling her a "fat cow" or "fat bitch." In September 1991, Harold took Betty outside, threw her to the ground, and tore open her blouse. He then grabbed a bottle of farm chemicals, poured it on her belly, and rubbed it in violently.

> "Maybe this will help you lose some weight! I'll burn some of this fat off you!" he yelled.

Betty considered leaving him, but he threatened that if she ever did, he would hunt her down and kill both her and Heather. He said he would make her watch as he cut off Heather's fingers, joint-by-joint. Betty knew he meant it. Harold regularly carried a gun on his belt and often threatened to use it on her. He joked to a friend that he could chop up his wife and daughter and spread them all over the farm.

Betty was out of options. With nowhere left to turn, she put a gun to her own head with the intent of killing herself, but Heather stopped her. "What will happen to me if you do that?" Heather yelled at her mother for even thinking of leaving her alone with such a madman. Betty shot the revolver out the window in frustration.

That September, Betty was at a loss for a way out of her dreadful situation. On top of that, she was having debilitating migraine headaches. Betty saw a doctor when the headaches got so bad that she claimed she occasionally blacked out.

———

In the early morning hours of September 29, 1991, Betty was yanked out of bed and dragged down the basement stairs.

Harold was drunk and upset as usual, accidentally calling her "Pat," the name of one of his ex-wives. Harold was leaving for an antique show in Des Moines, Iowa, the next day and demanded that Betty help him pack boxes for the trip. He had also misplaced his wallet and demanded that she find it for him or she and Heather would be looking for it the whole next day, if necessary.

Annoyed that he had pulled her out of bed, Betty refused. She told him she was going back to bed and headed for the stairs. But before she reached the stairs, Harold pulled his gun on her. Betty froze for a beat, then lunged for the nearby workbench that had two revolvers on it. A .22 and a .38. In a blink, she grabbed them both, cocked the hammers, pointed them both at Harold, closed her eyes, and fired twice with each gun. Harold mumbled, "Why did you go and do that?" as he fell to the ground.

When Betty opened her eyes, her husband laid on the basement floor. All four shots hit Harold. One shot hit his neck, two shots punctured his heart and both lungs, and another hit his back. She knelt down next to her husband and wept while the blood drained out of him.

Betty woke in a daze the next morning in her own bed. She was unsure what had happened the night before, initially thinking it was just a bad dream. However, a quick look down the basement stairs reminded her it was real. Very real. Her husband was dead. Betty closed the basement door and went about her day.

After seeing Heather off to school that morning. Betty drove 100 miles north to Cedar Rapids, Iowa, to take care of an insurance policy she had been working on. When she returned home that evening, she and Heather had dinner together and finished the day as if it were any other.

The following day, after Heather left for school, Betty returned to the basement. Psychiatrists would later say that what happened over the next six hours was the result of a "dissociative state" and an effort by Betty to avenge a lifetime of physical and mental abuse.

Using several knives and an electric circular saw, she got to work. She had butchered deer before, so she knew what to do. Betty began mutilating and dismembering her husband—starting with his genitals. She cut off his penis and testicles and placed them into a plastic bag. Using the circular saw, she cut off both legs—first at the knees, then the hip. Without the weight of the legs, she dragged the body to the garage where she cut off the arms.

Betty stripped the muscle and flesh from several of the limbs and cut the meat up into manageable bits. The heart, liver, and one lung were removed.

Using Heather's little red wagon, she piled the smaller parts of Harold's body onto the wagon and dragged it in the autumn sun, throwing body parts and chunks of meat haphazardly around the farm. The larger pieces she piled into the trunk of her car, drove down the country roads, and threw them on the side of the road randomly.

That afternoon, Betty picked her daughter up from school and the two of them went to get their hair done. That evening, the two of them went out to dinner. Heather was completely unaware of what her mother had done.

———

Eight days had passed and Betty knew she couldn't wait forever. She would eventually have to report Harold missing and come up with a story. On October 8 she called police to report her husband missing. She told police he had left the farm on September 30 in a white van on his way to Illinois to take care of some antique business, but she hadn't heard from him since.

When police came to the farm to ask questions about his disappearance, it didn't take long to realize that something sinister had happened. Near the gate of the farm, they found a knife and a leather belt with the initials "HF" branded on it. As they questioned Betty, Heather walked in during the conversation with some information. She had called her cats in to feed them, but when they didn't come, she went looking for them. Police were a little shocked when she said she found her cats in a strawberry patch nearby, eating a rotting piece of fleshy meat.

A search team was brought to the Frieberg farm and scoured the property for the next two days. When they found a large bone and a shoe beneath netting used to cover hay bales, they knew they had a murder on their hands. They also found a right arm, a torso, and random body parts all over the farm. Police gathered various knives, the power saw, two rifles, a revolver, the life insurance policies, a rug containing a bullet, a bloody bath towel, and a file folder containing Harold's previous divorce documents. On October 10, police returned to arrest Betty Frieberg.

————

When confronted with the evidence against her, Betty quickly confessed to killing her husband, but pleaded inno-cent. She said the killing was in self-defense. She knew that if she hadn't shot, Harold would have killed her. That, of course, made sense. But what didn't make sense was why she dismembered and eviscerated his body, covered up the crime, and waited eight days to report him missing. Prosecutors wanted a quick case and offered a plea bargain, but Betty refused it, knowing it would mean a guaranteed life sentence.

The trial of forty-three-year-old Betty Frieberg drew significant media attention to the tiny town. If convicted, she would face life in prison. Betty had been charged with the murder, but not the mutilation of a corpse or concealing a crime. Because of this, her attorney reminded the jury that they were only there to determine if she had acted in self-defense. They weren't to take into consideration that she had butchered his corpse after death or lied to police about his disappearance.

The prosecution had tried to establish premeditation and argued that Betty had planned the murder. They pointed out that there were three life insurance policies totaling $250,000, of which she was the beneficiary. She had even sold them to him. However, a representative from the life insurance company testified that Betty would have known that if she caused a person's death, the policy wouldn't be paid.

Prosecutors explained to the jury that they agreed Harold was a chronic abuser, but despite the domestic abuse, Betty was not in a position to issue a death sentence to her husband for his crime.

Betty's lawyer, Tom Walter, was an eccentric six-foot-seven attorney that wore cowboy boots with his suit and carried a pink-haired Troll doll with him to trial each day. He explained to the media that it was given to him by his fifteen-year-old daughter for good luck. Ironically, Walter had represented Harold during one of his four divorces. Although he was from the small, rural area, he was well known in the state for arguing before the Iowa Supreme Court in a case that resulted in the state's sodomy laws being declared unconstitutional.

Walter called each of Harold's four ex-wives to the stand to testify about their abuse at the hands of Harold, but each time, the testimony was met with an objection by the prosecution. The wives were not allowed to testify, but it seemed as though the jury got the point. Walter told the court that it wasn't a case of battered-wife syndrome, but strictly a case of self-defense. Betty had killed her husband to avoid being killed herself.

Heather took the witness stand to describe her own abuses by Harold and the abuses she witnessed her mother receiving. Even a woman that was a customer buying antique furniture testified that she felt sorry for Betty when she came to their home. Harold had openly flirted with the woman in a crude way while berating Betty in front of her.

A psychiatrist that saw Betty shortly after the killing testified that he believed Betty was in a dissociative state when she dismembered her husband and was avenging her previous abuse. He hypothesized that when she cut off Harold's penis, she was specifically avenging the rapes she had endured as a child. He also believed that she dispensed of his body parts throughout the farm because Harold had said he would do the exact same thing to her.

The prosecution pointed out that the medical examiner determined that the first gunshot was to Harold's back, meaning that he couldn't have been pointing a gun at her. They also told the jury that no fingerprints were found on the gun that Betty claimed Harold had pointed at her and it also wasn't loaded.

Betty Frieberg & Tom Walker with his lucky Troll doll.

But none of that seemed to matter. The jury believed her and Betty Freiberg was acquitted of murdering her husband, Harold. After the trial, she spoke with the media clutching her lawyer's lucky Troll doll and said, "If I had known the gun he was holding was unloaded, we'd still be together. I still love him. I wish it hadn't happened. I wish I could have gotten help for both Harold and I. And I hope women don't ever have to go through what I went through."

At the time of this writing, Betty Frieberg still lives in the area around Libertyville and kept the surname Frieberg.

8

THE DINNER THEATER MURDER

Mike Miller and Steven Hricko had been lifelong friends since the seventh grade, growing up in State College, Pennsylvania. The two attended Penn State University and in 1984 Mike met Maureen, who would later become his wife. Maureen worked as a waitress at a steakhouse with another waitress named Kimberly. Kimberly was very outgoing and full of energy, so she and Maureen quickly became best friends. It wasn't long before Mike and Maureen thought it would be a good idea to play cupid and set up Kimberly and Steven on a blind date.

The two couples went on a double date and it was love at first sight. From the moment of the first date, Kimberly and Steven were inseparable. In March 1989 they were married. Mike was Steven's best man and Maureen was Kimberly's maid of honor. When Mike and Maureen were married just a few months later, the roles were reversed. Steven served as Mike's best man and Kimberly as Maureen's maid of honor. For years, the four of them spent as much time as they could together, even spending weekends and vacations together.

The life of the two couples seemed to be something out of a storybook.

Mike and Steven were both avid golfers and, throughout the years, both took jobs in the golf industry. Steven worked as a superintendent of golf courses for several golf clubs throughout Pennsylvania and Maryland, while Mike had a similar career which eventually took him to a golf course in Maryland.

Kimberly & Steven Hricko

After graduating from college, Kimberly Hricko gave birth to their daughter, Anna Rose, and began a career in the health-care field. Kimberly worked as a certified surgical technologist where she assisted with surgeries. One responsibility of her job was to dispose of unused pharmaceutical drugs following surgeries.

Although both couples lived in Maryland and kept in constant contact, they lived almost two hours from each other. By the summer of 1997, however, after eight years of marriage, Steven and Kimberly's marriage had lost its luster.

Kimberly felt that her life with Steven had become stagnant. She was still as energetic and active as ever, whereas Steven had become more of a homebody. She complained that he didn't take her on dates anymore and rarely bought her flowers like he used to. At thirty-two years old, Kimberly wanted more from life and she didn't keep it a secret. By the fall of 1997, she began telling several of her friends of her discontent.

She confided to a co-worker at the hospital where she worked that her marriage had been on the rocks for quite some time. Years, in fact. She admitted she was sometimes verbally abusive to Steven and demanded that he go to counseling. Not the two of them... just him. She said he needed to work on himself.

That November, Kimberly's friend, Jennifer Gowen, was planning her wedding and asked Kimberly to be the matron of honor. In the days leading up to Jennifer's wedding, again, Kimberly opened up about her unhappiness. She told Jennifer she was considering divorcing Steven.

A week before Jennifer's November 29 wedding, Kimberly hosted her bachelorette party and, days later, her bridal shower. Along with Thanksgiving Day, it was a full week of festivities. Jennifer's family came from out of town for the week of celebration, one member of which was her cousin Brad Winkler. Brad was a handsome, twenty-three-year-old United States Marine sergeant assigned to the Pentagon. Although he was ten years younger than she was, Kimberly instantly took an interest in the young man.

During the events of the week, Kimberly snuck off to have private conversations with Brad, who had just gone through a nasty breakup. His young marriage had ended in divorce and Kimberly lent a sympathetic ear. She wasn't hiding her flirtations, though. Her friends noticed it, Jennifer Gowen noticed it, and her husband noticed it.

Steven Hricko silently fumed with jealousy. He knew he was losing Kimberly. He had gone to counseling as she had asked, but that hadn't seemed to appease her. After the wedding, Steven tried desperately to win back the love of his wife, but what he didn't realize was that it was too late. By early December, she was having an affair with the young Marine.

Brad Winkler had stayed in town after the wedding to house-sit for Jennifer and her new husband while they were on their honeymoon. Kimberly had stopped by Jennifer's townhouse to check up on Brad every chance she got. Her friend's home became her and Brad's illicit sex hideout.

Even with an affair, Kimberly couldn't contain herself. She told Jennifer, her co-workers, and her friends, "I'm not going to marry this guy. This is just about sex." Although she had no intentions of marrying Brad, one thing she knew for sure was that she wanted out of her marriage to Steven.

———

The wheels were spinning out of control in Kimberly's head. She wanted a divorce, but she didn't want to risk losing custody of their daughter. There had to be another way.

In December 1997, Kimberly approached Kenneth Burges, another surgical technician that she worked with. Most of his co-workers knew that more than a decade earlier, he had been convicted of welfare fraud. In Kimberly's mind, his felony conviction meant he might be a likely candidate for what she had in mind. Facing away from him, Kim asked,

"Hey Ken, would you kill my husband for $50,000?"

Assuming she was joking, he laughed and said,

"Ha! You work in the operating room. You could just put him to sleep."

But when he turned around, he saw her face—he knew she was serious. He immediately declined her offer and was shocked that she would even ask. She then asked if he knew anyone that would do it for her and, again, he quickly scoffed, "No!" "Oh, okay. Well, forget about it. Please don't tell anyone I asked," she said before she walked away.

The more Kimberly thought about it, the more she became obsessed. Despite the idea being so absurd, it didn't stop her from telling her friends. At a New Year's Eve party, Kimberly revealed to her friend Theresa that she was angry and upset and wanted out of her marriage. So much so that she admitted she had been thinking of ways of killing Steve.

Kimberly spoke at length about her hatred of her husband while Theresa listened in disbelief. Surely it was all just talk. She asked Kimberly, "What would you get out of it?" Kimberly told her she and Anna could live life on their own, the way they wanted to live it, with the insurance money. Kimberly was the sole beneficiary of two of Steven's life insurance policies. Without her husband, she would be $450,000 richer.

For the next month and a half, Kimberly spoke nearly every day to Jennifer Gowen about her frustration with her marriage and the contempt she harbored for Steve. She shared details of her affair with Jennifer's cousin in Jennifer's home and confided that she had sex with Steven only once since November, and it made her want to throw up.

Initially she had only told Jennifer that she was considering divorce, but as time passed Kimberly shared that she had considered killing Steven or having him killed. In Kimberly's twisted mind, she tried to justify her thoughts of killing him. There was the issue of Anna. If they divorced, Steven might get custody of their only child. Even if they shared custody, she worried Steven might tell Anna things to drive a wedge between Anna and herself.

Kimberly even expressed her delusional opinion that Steven would actually be "better off dead." She reasoned he had no life outside of the family and a divorce would devastate him. She hypothesized Steven might even kill himself. Kimberly's rationalization was that if Steven ever found out about the affair she had with Brad, he "would get depressed or angry enough to kill himself." And more importantly, if he ended up committing suicide she couldn't collect on the two life insurance policies, both of which had a suicide exclusion.

Kimberly explained a case to Jennifer in which a woman had injected children with succinylcholine, a muscle relaxant commonly used during surgery to relax the trachea when a patient needed a tube inserted. The drug dissipates in the bloodstream within five seconds of injection, leaving it untraceable. Kimberly had access to the drug from the excess medications she was in charge of disposing of after surgery. It seemed that Kimberly had been thinking about Ken Burges' initial joking response to her murder-for-hire proposal.

But Kimberly needed validation. Although she didn't ask her directly, Kimberly needed Jennifer to support her in order to justify the very idea of killing her husband.

Kimberly claimed her brother would support her even if she had killed someone and that, if the roles were reversed and Jennifer ever killed someone, she would be right there by her side. The statement baffled Jennifer and she didn't give Kimberly a direct response. She did her best to just listen to her friend, not really thinking that Kimberly would ever follow through.

———

On the evening of January 30, Kimberly called yet another friend, Rachel McCoy, leaving a frantic message on her answering machine.

> "Call me as soon as you get in. I really need to talk to you. Please, please call me! I just really need to talk to you. Call me as soon as you get in."

When Rachel called back minutes later, Kimberly pleaded with her to come to her house,

> "Do you remember when I saved you in State College? I need you now. I need you to come here now."

Late that night, Rachel arrived at Kimberly's house to find her upset and drinking. In the living room of Kimberly's home, she told Rachel of her thoughts of using the drug to paralyze Steven to stop his breathing. She then explained that she could set the curtains on fire with a cigar or candle and Steven would die of smoke inhalation.

Rachel was stunned. She pleaded over and over with Kimberly and told her that her plan was preposterous and just wouldn't work. And it's no way to end a relationship. She flatly told her that she just needed to get a divorce. That's what normal people do. What she was suggesting was ludicrous. Her daughter, Anna, couldn't grow up without a father.

But Kimberly had what she thought was a legitimate justification for every one of Rachel's arguments. Kimberly explained she believed killing her husband would be "easier" than getting a divorce. Without giving a reason, she claimed Anna would be better off without her father.

Rachel tried to reason with her, telling her she couldn't just burn down her brand new townhouse. There was also the issue of the neighbors' adjacent townhouses. They shared adjoining walls; she would put other people's lives at risk. But Kimberly seemed to have an insane rationalization for every rebuttal. Kimberly replied that her neighbors were always awake and would call the fire department before the entire building burned down.

The two spoke in the living room until about 1:30 in the morning, before Kimberly excused herself to use the bathroom. Rachel felt assured that she had talked Kimberly down and she wouldn't kill her husband. However, when fifteen minutes had passed and Kimberly hadn't returned from the bathroom, she walked up the stairs to check on her. She found Kimberly standing in her bedroom, blankly staring at Steven as he slept. Rachel had no idea that Steven was in the house that night.

Rachel took Kimberly back downstairs and spent the next thirty minutes calming her down until she felt comfortable that Kimberly wouldn't be doing anything rash. At least, not that night.

———

Steven was desperate. He knew his marriage was on its last legs and he would need to work hard to fix it—if that was even possible. He would need to become more affectionate. More communicative. He was attending counseling sessions, as Kimberly had requested, but it didn't seem to make her feel any better. It was no secret that she had been flirting with other men. Her eye was wandering. Out of ideas, he called his friend Mike Miller.

Mike had been working at Harbortowne Resort in St. Michaels, Maryland. The cottages of the golf resort stood at Hambleton Point, next to the water where the Miles River opened into the Chesapeake Bay. It was an exclusive resort that was booked up well in advance, but Mike suggested he could get them reservations for a special Valentine's weekend that the resort had planned.

The weekend included two nights in a waterside cottage, complimentary champagne, and a special murder mystery dinner theater show. It was perfect. Steven and Kimberly could get away for the weekend and Steven could gain some points to try to rekindle their marriage.

When Steven announced to Kimberly that he had booked the weekend getaway, she was amazingly receptive. Steven wrote in his diary,

> "Life at home is improving and I am looking forward to
> Valentine's weekend at Harbortowne with Kim. She called
> twice today and said 'I love you' without my saying it first. I

was very happy. Kim and I have not made love yet and I want to, but I will wait as long as it takes. I love her. I believe I know what being in love really is. We have been married 9 years but I feel like we just started dating."

To Steven, it seemed that they were headed toward reconciliation. It appeared as though their relationship was taking a turn. Kimberly, however, spent the days before Valentine's day writing a love letter to Brad.

"I really wanted to give you all these gifts in person, but I guess the Pentagon had a different idea. I am so proud of what you do, so I'll just go on missing you. Have a nice weekend at home, baby. I look forward to seeing you soon. Happy Valentine's Day, sir. I love you so very much. Hugs and Kisses, Kim"

———

At 3:00 P.M. on Valentine's day, the Hrickos arrived at the Harbortowne Resort and checked into their room. The murder mystery show of the evening was entitled "The Bride Who Cried." It was the tragic story of a groom who drank poisoned champagne at his own wedding reception. Dinner guests were invited to participate to help solve the mystery. Kimberly, in her usual form, was friendly and sociable, speaking to other dinner guests and actively trying to solve the mystery. The production ended near 10:30 P.M. and Kimberly and Steven retired to their cottage.

———

At 1:20 A.M., Kimberly Hricko parked her car in front of the hotel. She turned off the ignition and headlights, closed the door, and walked into the lobby. She held her mobile phone upside down to her ear, as if she were only listening to something rather than speaking to someone. "I need to speak to someone who works here," she said to a group of people gathered in the lobby. When an employee approached her, she calmly said, "I think my room is on fire." Her voice and actions showed no sense of excitement or urgency.

When the employee asked for her room number, she didn't know it. After looking her name up in the hotel registry, they realized she was in cottage 506 and the employee called 911. There was no mention of Steven until the 911 dispatch asked if there was anyone else in the room. "My husband could be in there," she replied.

Before emergency crews arrived, hotel employees rushed to the room and found the rear sliding glass door unlocked. Through the smoke, Philip Parker, an employee of the resort, saw there were human legs lying between the two twin beds. Keeping low to the ground, he crawled to the legs and pulled the body of Steven Hricko from the room. The top third of Steven's body, from his chest up, had been burned beyond recognition. His pajama pants were pulled down slightly. He was clearly dead.

———

A little over an hour later, Maryland State Police questioned Kimberly. She claimed that after leaving the dinner theater, she and Steven purchased four bottles of beer from the hotel bar before going back to their room. She said that Steven had drunk the bottle of champagne earlier in the evening and the four beers afterward while he smoked cigars and they watched "Tommy Boy" on the television. Kimberly told police that Steven had too much to drink and when he pressured her for sex, she refused and they started arguing. The argument only lasted ten minutes before she left the room and went for a drive in the car.

Despite it being near 11:00 P.M., she told police she drove toward the home of their friends Mike and Maureen Miller, who lived fifteen minutes away. She claimed she got lost, asked for directions several times, and finally found her way back to the hotel two hours later. When she returned to the room, she realized she had forgotten her key card. She went to the back sliding glass door and noticed the smoke from the fire. She told police she rushed back to the hotel lobby to get help.

———

Steven's body had been on the floor between the two twin beds along with two pillows under his head. A Playboy magazine laid nearby. Investigators found empty beer bottles in the garbage and on the nightstand next to the burned mattress. A package of Backwoods Cigars had one cigar missing. These findings initially confirmed Kimberly's story, but they didn't have to look very much further to find inconsistencies.

The fire was contained mostly to the mattress and the floor at the side of the bed where Steven had been laying. The rest of the room had minimal damage. Because the cottage had been well insulated, the fire didn't have enough oxygen to spread and had quickly extinguished itself.

Although it appeared that the fire had been caused by the lit cigar catching a pillowcase on fire, there was no evidence of the missing cigar. There was no butt or ashes anywhere in the room. The pillowcases had also been treated with flame retardant chemicals. Tests using the same brand of cigars and the same pillowcases proved it was impossible for the cigar to ignite the pillowcase without an accelerant of some kind. The hotel bedding and the mattress contained the same fireproof fabrics.

Fire Marshalls had eliminated any chance of an electrical fire. There was no chance of the fire being caused by faulty lights or heating. Accelerant sniffing dogs found evidence of a flammable liquid used on the floor where Steven had been laying, but they were unable to identify specifically what was used. That meant that they could not use any evidence of an accelerant in court. Regardless, the official cause of the fire was ruled to be arson.

In the days following Steven's death, Kimberly called the State Police investigator repeatedly asking if the Medical Examiner's report had been filed. She was anxious for an outcome. As she and family members prepared for a funeral, Kimberly's concern was not on the arrangements, but more so on making sure the body would be cremated rather than buried. She claimed it was what Steven had wanted.

————

Investigators questioned Kimberly's story. When an autopsy was performed on Steven's body, it became evident that she was lying.

Tests done on Steven's blood showed a normal carbon monoxide level in his system. Typically, someone involved in a fire will have a high level of carbon monoxide. Even more puzzling, his lungs and airways showed no sign of soot at all. This meant that Steven had not been breathing at the time of the fire. He was either already dead when the fire started, or someone had used a drug like succinylcholine to relax his muscles enough for him to cease breathing.

Kimberly's story started to fall apart when she claimed Steven had been drinking heavily that evening. The autopsy revealed a 0.00% level of alcohol in his system. He literally had no alcohol at all.

A quick questioning of friends and family confirmed that Steven rarely drank alcohol. On the rare occasion he drank, it was never in excess. He had been working hard to reconcile with his wife. He would not have picked that specific night to get hammered. Friends also confirmed that Steven never smoked—cigars or otherwise. In fact, he loathed them.

Kimberly, of course, disagreed with the evidence that piled up against her. She admitted that she and her husband had been having marital problems, but denied having anything to do with his death. However, when detectives found out that she had been having an affair and that Steven had $450,000 in life insurance with her listed as the beneficiary, her motives became obvious.

———

Despite the seeming mountain of evidence against her, building a case against Kimberly Hricko proved arduous. Prosecutors were unable to use any evidence of an accelerant being used in the fire and if she *had* used succinylcholine, any evidence would have been broken down by human enzymes in the body within seconds of injection. Also, the drug was not tracked and accounted for like a narcotic or other drugs would have been. She could have easily obtained it without any detection.

Investigators visited twenty-six convenience stores near the Hrickos' home to find where she had purchased the cigars. Incredibly, a store clerk remembered selling her the cigars and beer because she remembered commenting on Kimberly's distinctive red hair. The ink of the price sticker on the pack of cigars was also tested to further prove that they had been purchased at that particular convenience store.

Three months after the murder, Kimberly Hricko was arrested and charged with first-degree murder and first-degree arson. She pleaded not-guilty.

————

In court, the prosecution used a process called "conclusion by exclusion." By excluding all other possibilities of a fire starting in the room without the use of accelerant and Steven not breathing during the fire, they argued that the only other answer was that Kimberly had used a drug to incapacitate her husband and used a flammable liquid to start the fire.

The defense argued that Stephen could have lost consciousness from an accumulation of chemicals used at his work at golf courses. It was an unlikely scenario that still didn't explain how the fire had started.

Several of Kimberly's closest friends testified against her at trial, including Rachel McCoy, Jennifer Gowan, and Kenneth Burges. Each testified that Kimberly had told them of her premeditation and detailed the way she had planned to kill her husband. Unfortunately, each of them didn't think she was serious or capable of such a horrendous, senseless act.

Kimberly Hricko

In March 1999 Kimberly Hricko was found guilty and sentenced to life in prison plus thirty years. Due to advancements in technology, succinylcholine can now be identified in a human body.

The murder mystery dinner theater plays continued at the Harbortowne Golf Resort. Cottage 506 was booked far in advance for the next several years by people excited to stay in the room where Kimberly Hricko killed her husband.

9

MOMMY'S LITTLE HELPERS

Hilma Marie Witte was just eight years old in the mid-1950s when her family moved to a nudist camp in Del Ray Beach, Florida, just north of Miami. Her mother, Margaret O'Donnell, and step-father managed the camp for several years, where people could pay for admission and feel free to be themselves.

Just a few years earlier, Margaret had lost custody of her two young daughters briefly when she was admitted to a mental hospital for emotional problems. However, their new life in the nudist camp appeared to change her outlook.

When Hilma turned sixteen-years-old she married a young man from the camp in a nudist wedding. Despite being underage, Margaret sold admission to the camp as usual and allowed patrons to take photos of the wedding. Some photos made their way into a nudist magazine, but that didn't seem to bother her mother.

Hilma's marriage didn't last long, but she soon met another man at the nudist camp, Paul Witte. Paul was a large, burly man, ten years older than Hilma. He loved the outdoors and enjoyed fishing and hunting. Paul and Hilma were married and moved to another seaside town much further north: Beverly Shores, Indiana.

Paul Witte worked as a mill worker and a volunteer fire-fighter in northern Indiana. Hilma and Paul had two sons, Eric and John, and as soon as they were old enough, he took them out camping, hunting, and fishing. Though he tried his best to be a loving husband and father, he had anger issues and his idea of discipline was extreme. Hilma and the young boys were often beaten at the hand of Paul Witte.

Ever since Eric could remember, he had been beaten by his father. Eric was the elder of the sons and Paul felt he needed strict discipline in order to become a strong man. Though John was abused too, he didn't receive quite the same treatment as his older brother.

Hilma was a target of Paul's abuse as well, but when Paul went after Eric, she would get out of the way. Hilma would hide in another room of the house until the punishment was done for fear that if she intervened or tried to stop him, she would become the target. After each beating, when Paul had left the room, Hilma stepped in to comfort her crying son.

Although he appreciated the soothing sympathy of his mother, Eric's world changed one day when he was eight years old. His father had whipped and beaten Eric particularly brutally after he caught Eric in a lie about his grades. Afterwards, as his mother iced his wounds, she whispered a shocking thought to her son,

> "You can't keep going through this. He has to be stopped. Wouldn't it be better if he was dead?"

The boy didn't know how to respond to such a suggestion.

In the days following the beating, Eric's bruises were still sore to the touch. At school, he was embarrassed to show his face that had obvious shades of purple. While Paul was away at work, Hilma sat down with Eric and made it known to him she was serious. "We need to do something. If you were to do it… how would you do it?" Again, Eric didn't know how to respond, but Hilma had some ideas of her own. She told Eric she would try to poison his father. It was all for the good of the family.

In the past, Paul had an adverse reaction to the sedative Valium and his doctor suggested that he may be allergic to it. Knowing this, Hilma began feeding him valium in his food and disguised in the daily vitamins that he took. When he didn't react, she gradually increased the dosage. However, each time he had no reaction other than drowsiness.

When the Valium didn't work, she began using rat poison that contained arsenic. Any chance she got, Hilma put small amounts of the poison in his food and vitamins. Over the course of several years, she continued increasing the dosage, but Paul still had little reaction other than becoming sick. Perhaps she fed it to him so gradually that he had slowly built up a tolerance.

By the time Eric was fifteen, Hilma had put more and more pressure on him to "do something" about his father. He was the recipient of most of Paul's anger and she suggested he take matters into his own hands to save the family. She couldn't do it herself.

By the summer of 1981, Hilma had put together a plan to kill her husband. She convinced Eric that if he shot his father, he would be tried as a juvenile. She told Eric that by the time he reached eighteen, he would be released and they would be free of Paul's abuse.

Hilma supplied Eric with a handgun and told him to hide behind the front door and wait for Paul to come home from work, then shoot him as he walked in. The obedient boy did as his mother told him and hid behind the door with his stomach in knots. When his father walked in the door, Eric stood frozen. Without seeing Eric, Paul walked to the couch and laid down.

Eric was still frozen behind the door, unable to move. When he finally heard his father snoring, he lost his nerve and walked away. He couldn't do it. Fear kept him from pulling the trigger. He explained to his mother that he had failed, but Hilma was undeterred, telling him, "We'll try again later."

Hilma hadn't told Eric, but time was quickly running out. She and Paul had received a bank loan to buy new furniture. Paul repeatedly asked her when the furniture would be delivered, but Hilma always had an excuse for the delay. The truth was, she had spent the money on herself. Eventually, he was going to find out.

Hilma couldn't lie to her husband forever and told Eric it was now or never. She told Eric that if he didn't kill his father, she would commit suicide and leave him and his brother to be raised by their father. On September 1, 1981, Hilma left the house and told Eric she wouldn't return until Paul was dead.

Eric sat alone in his bedroom, brooding over what to do as his father lay asleep on the living room couch. Hilma called her son one last time. "Is it done?" She asked. Eric again said he couldn't do it, but Hilma threatened,

"I am coming home in fifteen minutes. If he's not dead when
I walk in that door, I'm leaving tomorrow and you'll never
see me again!"

Eric sat distressed for several minutes before he walked into
the living room with the gun in his hand. He watched as his
father slept on the couch. Through the front window, he
could see the headlights of his mother's car pulling up the
driveway. Eric walked up behind his father and shot him in
the head.

Almost immediately after he fired the shot, Hilma walked in
the front door to console her son, who was shaking in fear.
He had done as she'd asked. Hilma quietly calmed him, then
picked up the phone and called 911. Waiting for police to
arrive, she told Eric to stick to her story. She instructed him
to tell police he had found a gun and went into the living
room to show his father. When he tripped on the rug, the
gun went off, hitting his father in the head. It was a believable story. The house was cluttered and unkempt. Again, Eric
did exactly as his mother told him.

Eric repeated the lie to detectives. A brief investigation
ensued and it was determined that it was simply an accident.
Eric had accidentally shot his father and no charges were
filed.

Eric missed his father, but he felt no guilt for what he had
done. At just fifteen years old, with the coaxing of his
mother, he believed killing his father was the only option he
had to live a normal life.

———

After Paul's death, his elderly mother, Elaine Witte, invited the family to move in with her. She had always liked Hilma and thought of her daughter-in-law as the daughter she never had. Both of the boys enjoyed living with their grand-mother, who had no idea that they had plotted and killed her own son.

Hilma, Eric, and John lived with Elaine for three years until seventy-four-year-old Elaine noticed that her Social Security checks were mysteriously disappearing from the mail. Elaine confronted Hilma about the missing money, but she denied knowing anything about it. Hilma, however, had actually been intercepting the checks, forging Elaine's signature, and cashing them for herself.

The tension was growing in the Witte household when Eric noticed his mother doing something familiar. She was mixing something into Elaine's food. Eric knew what that meant and confronted his mother. He was angry. He felt he had killed his father out of necessity. The man was beating the family senseless. It was justified. He believed that if he hadn't killed his father, eventually his father would have killed one of them. But Elaine… she was just a nice older lady. As sweet as could be. She did not need to die. Hilma disagreed.

Hilma, John, & Eric Witte

His mother again spoke incessantly to both of the boys about getting rid of their grandmother, but Eric didn't want to hear it. At eighteen-years-old, Eric had very few options, but he knew one thing—he had to get away. If his mother was determined to kill Elaine, he didn't want to be a part of it. In the summer of 1983, Eric enlisted in the United States Navy and left for boot camp in San Diego, California. However, Eric's mother wasn't going to let him get out of it that easily.

Just weeks after Eric left for boot camp, Hilma worked her manipulation skills on her younger son, fourteen-year-old John. She told John that because his brother Eric wasn't there to do it, he had to kill his grandmother, Elaine. John spent the night in his grandmother's basement smoking pot and drinking himself into a stupor, anguishing over what he would have to do the following day.

On January 8, 1984, John Witte snuck into his grandmother's bedroom and shot her in the ribcage with a medieval crossbow as she slept. The single shot killed her instantly.

Within hours, with Elaine still dead in her bed, John and Hilma took a train to Chicago, where she was due to appear in court. She was trying to get Paul's disability benefits.

———

Hilma was able to convince the Navy to let Eric come back to Indiana before he even finished boot camp, explaining that there was a family problem. When Eric arrived back home, his mother took him into the basement. A freezer stood in the corner with chains and locks, keeping it tightly closed. Hilma opened the freezer to show her son what they had done.

The body of Elaine Witte had been reduced to small bits that fit into plastic trash bags. Hilma and John had spent the past week cutting up and disposing of Elaine piece by piece. The contents in each bag barely resembled anything human. They had dismembered the major joints using a chainsaw, hand saws, knives, and chisels. They flushed as much as they could down the toilet and the garbage disposal, then microwaved others into unrecognizable parts. Many parts were cooked in the oven and a deep-fat fryer. Others had been dissolved with acid in the bath tub. The remaining pieces were placed into the bags, mixed with dirt to make them further unrecognizable, and frozen.

Eric was in shock at what he saw, but his mother blamed him. It was all his fault. She told him that when he left for boot camp, he left the family without a better solution. Now she needed him to fix the situation – a situation that had gone wrong in so many ways.

Eric was at a loss. Not knowing what to do, he told his mother to tell Elaine's friends and family that she had gone on a long vacation. It was a temporary fix at best and no proper solution at all.

Trying yet again to distance himself from his mother's craziness, Eric drove back to San Diego with his friend, Doug Menkel. But by the time they reached Tennessee, they noticed a putrid smell and flies buzzing around a large cooler his mother had placed in the back of his truck. When Eric opened the cooler, hundreds of maggots covered black plastic bags with Elaine's remains inside. Hilma had given her son a macabre parting gift.

Scared to dump the bags along the way, Eric instead drove all the way to San Diego with them, rented a storage locker, left the bags there, and went back to boot camp.

Back in Indiana, Hilma enlisted the help of her mother, Margaret, while John recruited a friend to help get rid of the remaining body parts. The real problem, however, was Elaine's friends. They were growing impatient and didn't believe Hilma's story about Elaine being on vacation.

Eight months had passed since Elaine's death and Hilma didn't miss a beat, forging her signature and cashing Elaine's Social Security checks. Eventually Elaine's friends went to police and reported her missing. The detective assigned to the case was the same one that took the statement from Eric after his father's death. Just three years after an accidental shooting, another family member mysteriously went missing. The detective thought it was suspicious.

With Elaine's friends and family constantly questioning her and law enforcement closing in, Hilma and John fled to San Diego. Hilma planned to pick up Eric and the three of them would cross the border into Mexico. It wasn't to be, though. On November 7, 1984, Hilma and John were taken into custody in Chula Vista, California, trying to cash one of Elaine's Social Security checks. Eric was arrested later in the day at the Naval Hospital in San Diego.

Fifteen-year-old John was the first to break. He confessed to killing his grandmother with the crossbow and cutting up her body. By that time, however, there was nothing left of Elaine. The pieces of her body had been disposed of in random locations throughout Indiana, Illinois, and a landfill in San Diego. Initially, Eric did just as his mother requested and denied everything. Detectives also arrested Hilma's mother, Margaret, and Eric's friend, Doug Menkel, who both confessed to their involvement.

Eventually, Eric took a plea deal. Both Eric and John were convicted of voluntary manslaughter and sentenced to twenty years in prison. Both were released after eleven years.

Hilma denied involvement in either crime and pinned the blame on her boys. She claimed John had killed his grand-mother because he was obsessed with the game Dungeons and Dragons, but the court didn't buy her story. In 1986, Hilma Marie Witte was sentenced to a total of ninety years in prison for murder and conspiracy to commit murder. She was also convicted on several forgery and conspiracy counts in California for cashing Elaine's Social Security Checks.

Hilma has been denied parole twice as of the time of this writing. She will be eligible for parole again in 2028.

10

THE LLAMA FARM MURDER

O n the afternoon of April 18, 2016, Diane Walker contacted the Milford, Pennsylvania police to report her seventeen-year-old daughter, Leanna, missing. Initially, police were unconcerned. They knew she wasn't kidnapped; she left of her own accord. In the prior weeks, Leanna had mentioned to friends and family of her intentions to run away with her boyfriend, twenty-four-year-old Sky McDonough.

Leanna's friends thought she was crazy to even suggest she would run away with McDonough. Not only was he seven years older than Leanna, but he was creepy, to say the least. Her friends described him as "a bit off in the head."

Leanna Walker & Sky McDonough

As far back as high school, classmates had noticed Sky McDonough's strange behavior. When someone had mentioned to him that he had bad breath, he picked up dirt from the ground and ate it, claiming that soil from the earth was all that one needed to rid the body of toxins like the germs that cause bad breath.

On McDonough's Facebook page, he professed himself to be a Rastafarian—a religion developed in Jamaica with the belief that a God named Jah resides within every individual. The religion emphasizes natural living, specific dietary requirements, wearing the hair in dreadlocks, and includes the smoking of marijuana as a sacrament.

McDonough came across as a typical all-American clean-cut young man, nothing that would even slightly resemble a stereotypical Rastafarian. He mostly enjoyed the part that emphasized smoking weed and was once arrested for possession of drug paraphernalia.

His views on religion, however, were obsessive and skewed to his own liking. On Facebook, he posted loose interpretations of biblical quotes and two-hour videos of religious readings that he believed to be "lost books" of the Bible.

His own beliefs were perhaps drug-induced. He believed God didn't like tattoos and would banish a person to hell for having them. He believed men should marry young and have many wives. He often quoted passages from the Bible that suggested if a man's wife ever leave him, he should kill her.

***

Leanna Walker and Sky McDonough met in January 2016 through a mutual friend and, despite their age difference, the two began dating. Almost immediately McDonough became possessive of Leanna and began calling her his "wife."

Leanna was in her junior year at Delaware Valley High School, but McDonough couldn't stand that she was around other boys at school all day without his supervision. It drove him crazy and he let her know. At McDonough's request, Leanna dropped out of school and enrolled online to study for her high school equivalency exam. Anything to keep her new boyfriend happy and appease his jealousy.

By February, McDonough found himself without a place to live. Leanna's mother, Diane, didn't approve of the age difference between her daughter and McDonough, but she felt sorry for the young man. Although she didn't know him well, she allowed him to stay in a room at their home. It would only be temporary—until he got back on his feet again.

Over the next several weeks, Diane got a clear view of what kind of person Sky McDonough really was. Living with him in the house was pure insanity. His moods were prone to sudden and unpredictable changes. At times, he was violent and threatening. He was clearly not mentally stable, but his control over her daughter was overwhelming. Leanna was in love. There was no stopping it.

He had spent over two weeks in their home, but when McDonough told Diane that if Leanna ever left him, he would "burn the whole family down," it was more than she could take. She called the police and had McDonough forcibly removed from their home.

By March, however, McDonough's strange behavior had escalated and he was admitted to Bons Secours Community Hospital in Port Jervis, New York, as a psychiatric patient. Due to closed medical records, it isn't clear exactly why McDonough had been admitted, but he spent the majority of March in the hospital. Diane Walker forbade her daughter from visiting him during his stay. However, as soon as he was released, Leanna wired him money for a bus ticket back to Milford.

Although McDonough was no longer welcome in the Walker's home, Leanna's younger brother called his mother when he saw McDonough and Leanna together in the house. When Diane Walker got home on the afternoon of April 18, both he and Leanna were gone. They had run away together. Diane had no idea she would never see her daughter alive again.

———

On the day he and Leanna disappeared, McDonough changed his Facebook profile image to a black-and-white photo of himself hugging Leanna from behind, his hands across her breasts as he kissed her on the cheek. Diane had reported her daughter missing as a runaway, but several days had gone by and she'd heard nothing from her daughter. That wasn't like her. She would have called. Leanna would have known that her family was worried sick. Diane pressured the police to change the case from a runaway to a kidnapping. She told police that Sky McDonough had threatened their life in the past and she was worried that he might have done something terrible to Leanna.

For days, police searched the dense forests of the area using helicopters and dogs, but found nothing.

Eight days had passed since Leanna had gone missing. On April 26, Sky McDonough was spotted in New Jersey after a warrant for his arrest had been issued in the state on burglary and trespassing charges. He had been breaking into homes—stealing food to survive in the week since he and Leanna had been gone.

By April 26, he had made his way back to Milford and ran into a friend at a supermarket. McDonough bragged to the friend that he was wanted by police and had been living in the woods with a girl. That friend, however, immediately called police to report his location. When police approached McDonough, he ran. After being chased and tased, he was arrested, but there was no sign of Leanna. He told police that he and Leanna had been camping and he had given her instructions to run away if he didn't return soon.

Officers demanded that McDonough show them where they had been camping. He led police to a dense wooded area north of Milford on Foster Hill Road where he had worked at a nearby llama farm.

McDonough knew the forest around the llama farm well. He knew the trails, he knew the hills, and he knew places to hide. Trudging through the woods for hours, police realized he had been leading them around in circles. When McDonough saw his chance, he ran again.

Sky McDonough & His Facebook Profile Update Photo

Still handcuffed and shirtless, McDonough ran deep into the woods. Local Milford Police called in Pennsylvania State Police to help search the llama farm for him. Just before noon the following day, McDonough was again taken into custody.

As police searched for Leanna, McDonough sat in jail and told police,

> "We ran away together. That's it. I didn't hurt her. We went to the llama farm and then afterwards I went to get a check and I got caught by police. I don't know what happened to her."

Friend and Family Helping in the Search / McDonough Waves for the Cameras

Search and rescue crews searched the llama farm using helicopters and sniffer dogs. Almost three weeks into the search, dogs found human remains in a shallow grave. It was the body of Leanna Walker. She had been burned and buried deep in the forest under about eight inches of soil. The Pike County coroner determined she had died of "homicidal violence with her body burned post mortem," but gave no further detail of exactly how she died.

McDonough had no explanation and claimed she must have been killed by someone else.

> "She's been hanging out with bad boys. She had some other guys that she was with."

McDonough, however, offered no description of who the "other guys" were, but he told police he believed they were most likely responsible for her death.

McDonough remained in police custody for over a year before charges were finally brought against him. He was charged with first-degree murder, kidnapping, interference with the custody of children, flight to avoid apprehension, and tampering with evidence.

Armed with a warrant, detectives searched Facebook messages that Leanna had with her friends and between herself and McDonough. The messages told of Leanna's fear and abuse. Just before her death, she wrote to a friend,

> "Sky's crazy he tried killing me and cops are trying to look for him and he's on his way to Jamaica cuz if cops find him, they're putting him in a mental hospital again."

Additional messages from before she disappeared showed that McDonough had beaten Leanna and threatened to kill her,

> "I was only going to kill you for running off with another man."

During interviews with his friends, a former co-worker at the llama farm, David Decker, told detectives that McDonough once shared that if Leanna ever tried to leave him, he would kill her and burn the body to cover up the smell. Ultimately, that was exactly what he had done.

Detectives also interviewed his cellmates while he was in jail. One confessed McDonough had told him, "Well, the blood is on her head because she wouldn't change her ways."

A prison guard told police that McDonough had theorized that,

"A bear may have got to her and ripped her up. And lightning burned her. She is cured and in a better place now."

McDonough denied having anything to do with Leanna's death until November 2018. Two and a half years after the murder, McDonough was offered a deal. In order to avoid a trial where his defense would most likely have used his history of mental illness to their advantage, prosecutors offered him a third-degree murder charge. McDonough pleaded guilty to third-degree murder, interference with the custody of children, escape, resisting arrest, and corruption of minors.

Sky McDonough admitted he had run away with Leanna and convinced her they could escape the United States and live happily in Jamaica. After several days of camping in the Pennsylvania woods, Leanna revealed she didn't want to go with him. She wanted to go home. This didn't sit well with McDonough. If he couldn't have her, no one could. Sky McDonough admitted he killed Leanna Walker, burned her body, and buried her in a shallow grave on the llama farm.

In Pennsylvania, third-degree murder is a catch-all that's similar to manslaughter in other states. Essentially, it's anything that does not fall under the definition of first-degree murder, which includes premeditation, or second-degree murder, which involves an accomplice.

McDonough was sentenced to twenty-one to forty-two years in prison, the maximum penalty allowed for a third-degree conviction.

11

A STAGED SCENE

With her father enlisted in the military, Lisa Dahm's family had moved around the globe throughout her life. However, just before Lisa graduated from high school in 1988, the Dahm family had settled in the area around Fort Lewis, just south of Tacoma, Washington. After graduating from high school, Lisa trained for a job in the healthcare field and was working as a nurse's aide by the early nineties.

Lisa worked in Puyallup, Washington, just south of Tacoma at Rainier Rehabilitation home; a long-term nursing home and short-term rehabilitation facility for disabled adults. It was there that she met Daniel Carlson in 1993.

Daniel Carlson was a quiet, twenty-one-year-old redheaded nurse. His mother, Carol, and his father, Daryl, also worked at the same nursing home: Carol in housekeeping and Daryl as an attendant counselor.

What started as innocent workplace flirtation between Daniel and Lisa eventually grew into love. They were an unlikely couple—Dan was a quiet and reserved small-town boy. Lisa was his first girlfriend. Lisa was outgoing and sociable, having traveled the world. Daniel adored the ginger-haired Lisa and within a year, the two married.

Just one year after they married, the couple were surprised when Lisa gave birth to twin boys, Nicky and Chris. They cherished the two young boys, but after two years, they were having trouble juggling work and paying to raise a family. By 1997, they decided Lisa would need to leave her job and become a full-time mother. It also meant that they would have to downsize and move to the suburbs.

Daniel and Lisa Carlson with their twin boys

Daniel's parents, Carol and Daryl Carlson, lived on a densely wooded plot of land in the tiny rural town of Kapowsin. The town sat thirty miles south of Tacoma, near the base of Mount Rainier, and was named after the Kapowsin Lumber Company that had operated a successful sawmill there in the early 1900s. Back then it was a bustling town with 10,000 residents, but by the early 1990s, long after the sawmill had closed, it was home to only about 300 people.

Carol and Daryl's home consisted of two trailer homes on a large piece of wooded property. They offered to let Daniel, Lisa, and the twins live in the extra trailer on the property. It was perfect for both Carol and Daniel. Carol wanted to spend more time with her grandkids and Daniel was a bit of a mama's boy. For Lisa, however, it was a nightmare. She had always lived in or near a big city. The extreme rural life was new for her and not very exciting.

Lisa and Daniel moved into the double-wide trailer in September 1997. The trailer sat about 150 yards from Carol and Daryl's home in Kapowsin, situated at the end of a long dirt road almost two miles from the nearest paved road. There were no street lights and the trailer had limited electricity that ran only a few hours per day. Although a thick wood divided it with no path from one home to the next, Carol could still see the windows of her son's new home.

Although they had cut back on their housing expenses, Daniel was just starting his career and his job simply didn't pull in enough money to support a family of four. He also had over ten credit cards he had maxed out. The interest alone was bleeding them dry. Lisa and Daniel fought almost daily over financial matters and how to raise their children. They also argued about Daniel's parents. Carol had become overbearing and regularly intruded into their personal and financial lives. She had an opinion about everything and always sided with her son in the event of arguments.

Through the years, Carol spied on Lisa and Daniel. Lisa had caught Carol peeking through their windows on more than one occasion until she finally had to keep the curtains closed. Each time Carol spied, she went home and made notes of what she saw. Carol could see that the strain on the marriage would eventually break and she was hoping to keep a record of what she believed was Lisa's lax parenting skills. She didn't have much faith in their marriage and knew that someday she could use those notes if the two divorced.

Soon after Lisa and Daniel moved to Kapowsin, one of Daniel's childhood friends, Shawn McKillop, started spending time with them. Daniel and Shawn had been friends since the sixth grade and Shawn was excited to see that his old friend was living so close again. Shawn introduced both of them to internet chat rooms, which were in their infancy at the time. Daniel didn't seem interested, but Lisa took to the chatrooms immediately. For her, it was something new and exciting that gave her something to do while at home all day with the kids.

Daniel's work schedule required that he work into the late evenings. Each afternoon, Lisa called her mother and told her how the kids were doing and how she was managing with her arguments with Daniel. She also vented to her mother about Daryl and Carol Carlson's constant meddling in their personal matters.

In the evenings Lisa logged on to the internet chatrooms and chatted with Shawn. She eventually opened up to him that she and Daniel were having marital problems and told him all the same things she told her mother. She told Shawn that her mother-in-law would frequently pop in uninvited. Lisa had to tell her repeatedly not to come over unannounced. She felt unsafe when she came out of the shower to find Carol waiting for her in her own bedroom.

Carol was overbearing and possessive of the twin boys and referred to them as "my babies." The boys were Carol's grandchildren, not "her babies", and the choice of term she used made Lisa uncomfortable. Carol wanted to play a role in every part of the young boy's lives and made it clear that she believed Lisa was not raising the boys in the right manner.

As her relationship got worse and worse with Daniel and his parents, her relationship with Daniel's childhood friend, Shawn, blossomed. She was lonely in the deep woods of Kapowsin. Her relationship with Daniel had gotten to the point where they weren't even speaking and he occasionally hit her. When it was obvious that her marriage to Daniel was beyond repair, she began spending more and more time with Shawn and eventually the two fell in love. Not wanting to hide it from Daniel, she let him know it was over and that she was having a relationship with Shawn.

In November 1997, Shawn helped Lisa write a separation agreement that Daniel and Lisa both signed. The agreement stated that Lisa would care for the kids during the day while Daniel was at work. Daniel generally left for work in the early afternoon and would return home by 11:00 P.M. When Daniel returned home from work, Lisa would go to Shawn's house.

The arrangement didn't sit well with Daniel's mother, Carol. She stepped up her spying tactics and began peeking in the windows again while Lisa would watch the kids. In February 1998, Carol's blood boiled when she saw Shawn's car in the driveway of their home. She stormed in the door screaming, "Whore! You little bitch! How could you do this to my son?!" Seconds later, Daniel's father, Daryl, burst in the door, hit Shawn, and grabbed Lisa by the throat. Daryl had expected to find them both naked after having sex, but they had only been sitting watching television. When he realized this, he released his grip on her throat and left. Because of the incident, Lisa got a restraining order against Daryl Carlson.

That April, Lisa and Daniel's financial situation had reached a crisis level. They were at risk of losing their car and having Daniel's wages garnished. They had no choice but to file for bankruptcy. The restructuring of debt, however, didn't relieve the stress between Lisa and Daniel and it seemed to only make matters worse between Lisa and Carol.

In mid-July, Lisa told a close friend she was planning on leaving Daniel. She planned to take the kids to Arizona where Shawn had family. She told the friend that she had mentioned it to Daniel and he exploded in anger, but she couldn't wait any longer. Once the bankruptcy was finalized in three days, she was filing for divorce.

The next day Lisa arrived at their Kapowsin home at 1:30 P.M. Thirty minutes later, Daniel called his work to let them know he was running late. He arrived at work at 3:00 P.M.

Carol Carlson spent the day at home and called her sister in the early afternoon to cancel plans they had for later in the day.

According to Carol Carlson, the three-year-old twin boys showed up in her front yard at 5:45 P.M. having walked from their parent's trailer. When Carol asked where Lisa was, the boys told her she was sleeping.

Carol called the other trailer and left messages for Lisa, but they went unanswered. After running errands early that evening, Carol returned home at 8:04 P.M. but there was still no word from Lisa. That was when she paged Daniel and told him he needed to come home to check on Lisa.

Daniel left work and conspicuously made a point to tell three co-workers he was leaving work early. He needed to find out what was going on with his wife. He returned to Kapowsin at 8:30 P.M. and entered through the front door of their home to find Lisa lying face-up on the couch with a blue blanket covering the lower half of her body. She had been shot and was covered in blood.

When Daniel called 911, he spoke in a strange monotone and initially could not remember his own address, his mother's phone number, or the color of either house. He was feigning shock. Then, in a calm voice that showed no signs of distress, he described the scene to the operator. When police arrived, they removed Daniel from the home and investigated the scene.

There was no sign of forced entry. Someone had shot Lisa twice in the head and once in the chest. The first shot to her head incapacitated her. The couch that she laid on was covered in blood and blood spray covered the wall behind the couch.

Beneath the large blanket covering her lower body, Lisa's pants had been pulled down to her ankles. They had been pulled rather than pushed—an indication that someone other than herself had removed the pants. On her right thigh was a vibrator covered in blood. The top of the vibrator had a cord which led to a control box in Lisa's hand. Blood covered both the control box and the vibrator, but since the first shot had incapacitated her, it was impossible that she would have gotten blood on the sex toys herself. Someone had placed them there.

The television was on with a pornographic VHS video tape paused on the screen. But the VCR was of the type that if a tape had been playing, it would have played until the end and rewound itself. It wouldn't have paused by itself. It was clear that someone had staged the scene in an attempt to degrade her – someone that had a deep hatred of her.

A bloody handprint smeared on the back of the couch showed that someone had moved her body after death into a lying position at the far right end of the couch. From the spray patterns on the wall behind the couch, it was obvious that she had been shot while in an upright position at the opposite end of the couch.

In the bedroom and bathroom, drawers had been pulled from cabinets and items tossed throughout the room, but jewelry boxes and jewelry in plain sight had not been touched. Nothing in the home was missing. It was clear that it was made to look like a robbery, but whoever had done it hadn't thought the crime through very well.

Outside, Daniel was questioned by police several times. The entire time, Daniel had a nervous smile and kept very little eye-contact with officers. Police noticed that he seemed very interested in clothes that he had left in the dryer, repeatedly asking if he could retrieve them. The clothes in the dryer contained a pair of Daniel's black pants, a white t-shirt, white men's underwear, black socks, and a towel. Forensic scientists later found blood and sperm on the items. They were unable to retrieve DNA from the items, but the blood type matched Lisa's.

During Daniel's initial questioning, he was asked if there was anything in the house that he believed would provide evidence. He told the detectives to listen to the answering machine.

When police examined the answering machine, they found three messages from Carol Carlson asking Lisa why the kids were at her house and why she was sleeping all day. The FBI, however, was later able to tell that another message from Lisa's mother had been erased. Lisa's mother had called several times to check up on her daughter. Carol had erased the message from Lisa's mother and recorded her own over the top.

When police examined Lisa's computer, there was evidence that it had been tampered with that afternoon. Someone had unsuccessfully tried to login into her rocketmail.com email account at 3:40 P.M. Daniel was at work by that time. Detectives believed Carol tried to access Lisa's account while she laid dead on the couch.

Detectives verified that Daryl Carlson had been at work the entire day, but Carol had been home and Daniel had a window of opportunity to murder his wife early in the afternoon before he left for work.

When police questioned Carol and asked why she hadn't simply gone to the trailer to check on Lisa, she claimed the twins had told her she was sleeping and she didn't want to wake her. Carol, however, told the local Fire Chief that she didn't go because Lisa had taken out a restraining order against her. She later told a detective that she wanted to "teach Lisa a lesson." Carol had trouble keeping her story straight and told her sister that the twins told her, "we had to run so the bad man doesn't get us too."

Carol's story of the twins walking to her house on their own was not a likely scenario. Although the homes were on the same plot of land, the area between them was dense brush and forest. The only way to get from one home to the other was down the long dirt driveways of each home. Two three-year-olds would have been unable to find their way to their grandmother's home on their own.

There was also the issue that Daniel had entered the house that night through the front door, when his usual entry would have been through the back door. Lisa was adamant about always locking the front door with the deadbolt and the chain. Daniel would have had no reason to enter through that door that night unless he knew it had been left unlocked.

Even more evidence came when they questioned Lisa's boyfriend, Shawn McKillop. Shawn supplied detectives with hundreds of pages of chat logs between Lisa and himself, where she spoke of her fear of both Daniel and Carol. He also supplied them with a cassette tape Lisa had secretly recorded of a conversation between herself and Daniel, where he admitted he had tried to strangle her.

Police examined the diaries that Carol kept after each time she spied on Lisa. From the notes she had taken, it was evident she was obsessed with Lisa. The notes detailed every fight that Daniel and Lisa had since they first moved into the trailer home. Each notation was worded in a way that showed her hatred of her daughter-in-law. From these notes, detectives could establish that Carol had a motive to murder Lisa. She was worried that Lisa was going to leave her son and gain custody of the two boys. She once told a co-worker there was "no way that bitch was ever going to take my grandkids away from me."

In the months after the murder, Daniel was worried that he would not be able to prove that he was at work when Lisa was killed. He confronted an employee of the Pierce County medical examiner's office and asked if there was a way to have the time of death altered on the death certificate.

———

Prosecutors took three years building a case against Carol and Daniel Carlson. In June 2001, they were both arrested and charged with first-degree murder as both principals and accomplices. They were also charged with a firearm enhancement for using a gun during the murder.

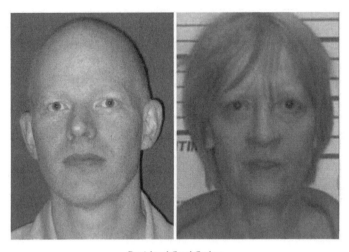

Daniel and Carol Carlson

Almost five years after the murder, Carol and Daniel were tried together. The defense portrayed Daniel as a heartbroken, loving husband and Carol as a simple-minded grandmother that didn't even know how to operate a computer.

Prosecutors had argued that Daniel killed his wife when she told him she was divorcing him and taking their kids to Arizona. Daniel then left for work to establish his alibi while Carol staged the scene with the vibrator, porn tape, and tried to make it look like a robbery. She then unsuccessfully tried to access her email to make it appear that Lisa was alive after Daniel had gone to work. She also altered the answering machine tape to establish her own alibi.

After much deliberation, a jury found them both guilty on all counts. Carol Carlson and Daniel Carlson were each given thirty-seven years in prison.

In 2006, however, both of their convictions were overturned on a technicality. A judge had determined that some of the evidence against them had been obtained illegally and portions of the testimony should not have been allowed by the judge. Rather than risk another trial, both Daniel and Carol were allowed to plead to lesser charges. Daniel pleaded guilty to second-degree murder and his sentence was reduced to twenty-three years, making him eligible for release in 2022. Carol pleaded guilty to three counts of second-degree assault and one count of sexually violating a corpse. She was sentenced to nine years in prison but was released early in 2008. One year after her release, she was diagnosed with cancer. She died the following year.

12

THE KILLER COP

Nancy Trotter was just seventeen years old when she met eighteen-year-old Paula "Sue" Wells in Chicago during the spring of 1972. Both girls had been hitchhiking across the country—Nancy from Detroit and Sue from Texas. They were both intent on seeing the world. However, after the cold Chicago winter, the young girls needed some sun. That June they stuck out their thumbs and worked their way down to Florida to work on their suntans.

The girls made their way to Stuart, a small town along Florida's Treasure Coast with a rich history of shipwrecked Spanish galleons and sunken gold and silver. The girls dropped their bags off at a youth hostel near the Martin county courthouse in the city center and asked for directions to the nearest beach.

Just a few miles away was Jensen Beach. It was the perfect location, with white sandy beaches that stretched for miles along the Atlantic Coast. It was a quiet beach and wasn't filled with tourists, like the beaches of Miami or Fort Lauderdale. Sunbathers and sea turtles peppered the coastline and the warm water was a perfect respite for the hot, humid summer.

On the morning of July 21, Nancy and Sue walked out of their hostel onto Ocean Boulevard and put out their thumbs in hopes of getting a ride to the beach. The first car to pull over, however, was a Sheriff's cruiser.

As the girls approached the car, an officer stepped out. "Hitchhiking is illegal, you know?" he said.

Although hitchhiking was extremely common in the 70s, it was technically illegal within Martin County. The girls explained they were just going a few miles away to Jensen beach and it was their only means of travel. The twenty-six-year-old introduced himself as Sheriff's Deputy Gerard Schaefer and offered to give the two young girls a ride to Jensen Beach.

During the short drive, Schaefer informed the girls of the dangers of hitchhiking. There were creeps and kidnappers out there, but the girls already knew that. Despite being young, the girls were street-wise, seasoned hitchhikers. After all, they had already traveled halfway across the country.

As they arrived at Jensen Beach, the officer offered to take them to the beach the following day, too. Just to be safe. Officer Schaefer seemed nice enough, the girls thought, and agreed to meet him the next morning at the park near the courthouse.

———

Gerard John Schaefer had been a recent recruit at the Martin County Sheriff's department and had only been employed there a month. He had previously been rejected by the Broward County Sheriff's Department after he passed their polygraph, physical exam, an IQ test, but failed a psychological exam. He had been employed briefly as a probationary patrolman for the Wilton Manor Police Department, but had been fired before his six-month probation had completed. His police chief cited the reason for his dismissal as a "lack of common sense" and "using poor judgement" when making arrests.

Prior to his law enforcement career, Schaefer had tried to enlist in the military four times. Each time he was rejected for "mental, moral, or physical" reasons.

Schaefer led a seemingly normal life according to acquaintances, friends, and family. His first marriage lasted only two years and in 1971, he married twenty-two-year-old Teresa Dean. His childhood was, by most accounts, relatively normal. There were no major family or school problems and throughout high school, he seemed to be just another young boy growing up in the sixties. After high school, he went to Florida Atlantic University and graduated with a degree in geography.

Although those around him believed Schaefer was a normal young man, he had obsessions that went largely unnoticed. In his late teens, he became fixated on women's panties and often peeked in women's bedroom windows.

Gerard Schaefer

Schaefer had confided to a childhood friend of his infatuation with his neighbor, Leigh Hainline Bonadies. As a teenager, he peeked in Leigh's window so often that he believed she was taunting him by undressing in front of her window. In September 1969, Leigh mysteriously disappeared. Schaefer was the last person to see her.

Officer Schaefer showed up right on time at the park by the courthouse to pick up Nancy and Sue. The girls were puzzled, however, when they saw he wasn't in his police cruiser. "Where's your police car?" The girls asked. Schaefer explained he was working as a "plainclothes" cop that day. His job was just to do observations. "It's sort of like undercover work," he lied.

The girls hopped into his blueish-green Datsun and Schaefer began driving toward the beach. As he drove, Schaefer again preached to the girls about the dangers of hitchhiking, while again the girls rebuffed his warnings.

He then asked about the hostel where they were staying. He said it was full of "Jesus freaks" and he had heard there were a lot of teenagers doing drugs there. He asked if they had encountered any drugs or drug trafficking, but they hadn't.

Before arriving at the beach, Schaefer excitedly asked the girls if they would like to see an old historic Spanish fort that was on a river. He touted its history and explained it was where Spanish boats came in during the 18th century. With no plans for the day other than laying on the beach, the girls said yes.

Schaefer drove an additional eight miles past Jensen Beach to an area on Hutchinson Island known as Blind Creek, where he pulled onto an overgrown dirt road. "Don't tell anyone I took you here," he said as he drove through the secluded jungle of palmetto palm trees and thick underbrush.

As he drove, he again spoke of the dangers of hitchhiking and told them, "I could dig a hole and bury you. There's no crime without a victim." The girls glanced at each other, but brushed off his blatantly inappropriate comment, assuming he was joking.

Just before they reached the old Spanish fort, Schaefer stopped the car, reached between the car seats, and pulled out two pairs of police handcuffs. "I've been instructed to arrest the both of you," he said. "You are runaways and we've been in contact with your parents." He pulled Sue out of the car first and handcuffed her, then Nancy.

Once handcuffed, Schaefer berated the girls, boasting at how easily he had kidnapped them. He told them he could easily sell them both into white slavery and fetch a nice profit for two young girls in their prime. "That would be a nice experience for you. You could really see the world!" he mocked.

Nancy mocked him back, "Yeah, yeah. Go get your sheikh and sell us."

The girls were still unafraid, knowing he was a cop. It had to all just be a joke. He went on chastising the girls, telling them he could dig a hole so deep for them they would be considered a missing person for the rest of their lives. "Would your parents put up a ransom for you?" he asked.

But the girls realized he wasn't joking when he walked to the back of the car, popped the trunk, and pulled out sheets, rags, and several lengths of heavy rope.

> "If I wanted to rape you, I could do it right here, right now!" he snapped. "If either of you run, I will kill the other one."

Schaefer wadded up a rag and stuffed it into Nancy's mouth. With her hands cuffed behind her back, he led her away from Sue to a fallen tree near the river bed. He forced her to stand on the fallen tree and, using a noose, tied her neck to the tree. Each time Nancy slumped forward, the rope around her neck choked her.

He then went back to Sue and laid her on a blanket, where he tied her feet together with rope and another around her shoulders. Using another length of rope, he tied a noose and threw it over the branch of a tree, then placed the noose around her neck. He instructed Sue to stand on a tree root as he tied the rope to a tree behind her. If she slipped from the root, she would hang. He told each girl that they had a decision to make. They needed to decide which one of them would die.

Suddenly Schaefer's police radio squelched. He was temporarily being called away, saving Nancy and Sue from their immediate doom. When he left, the girls both frantically tried to get untied without hanging themselves. Nancy spit the gag out of her mouth and managed to get part of the rope that was around her neck into her mouth. She chewed and chewed, at the same time trying to loosen the other ropes that held her to the tree. Eventually, she broke free and ran.

Nancy hid behind the old fort, unaware if Schaefer had known she had freed herself. She was unsure if he had returned. Then she heard Sue calling her name. Nancy's first instinct was to run and help her, but she was terrified that it could be a trap. Schaefer may have known that she escaped and was forcing Sue to call her name.

Nancy ran through the woods as fast as she could. When she thought she was far enough away, she hid in some thick brush. Although she was terrified of the spiders in the bushes, Schaefer scared her more. She laid silently. Every time a bird moved or the wind blew, she thought it might be him. She sat for a half hour until she was covered with mosquitoes and couldn't take any more. Again she ran, eventually reaching the river. With her hands still handcuffed behind her back, she swam through the river.

———

When Schaefer returned to the scene, he found both girls had freed themselves. They were gone and he knew he was in trouble. He searched the area, but there was no sign of either of the girls. He knew they would soon be found and report him, so he called his boss, Sheriff Crowder.

"I've done something stupid. I messed up. You're going to be mad at me," Schaefer told the Sheriff. He explained he had taken the two girls and tied them to a tree. He said he was trying to teach them a lesson on the dangers of accepting rides from strangers. He told the Sheriff that he was only trying to do the right thing, but Sheriff Crowder was furious. He instructed another deputy to take Schaefer into custody while he raced out to Hutchinson Island to look for the girls.

Sheriff Crowder quickly found both of the girls. One was still gagged and handcuffed, frantically running down the highway. The other he found wading in a shallow bay. Both had cuts and scratches all over their bodies from running through the heavy brush. He uncuffed both girls, wrapped blankets around them, and drove them back to Stuart.

Other than scratches, cuts, and a few jellyfish stings, the girls were physically okay. But they knew Schaefer's intentions were not merely to scare them; they believed he intended on raping and butchering them.

Paula "Sue" Wells and Nancy Trotter in a re-enactment of their abduction.

Gerard Schaefer was charged with abduction, imprisonment, and aggravated assault, but was quickly released on bail with his trial date set for four months later. That November at trial, prosecutors offered Schaefer a plea deal. If he pleaded guilty, he would only spend six months in the St. Lucie county jail. Schaefer jumped at the opportunity.

In addition to the light sentence, Schaefer asked for a bail extension. He explained to the judge that he needed time to help his wife move south to Fort Lauderdale with his mother. Since he was a former cop with no prior arrests, the sympathetic judge allowed Schaefer an extra two months before he needed to serve his time in jail. But Schaefer had much more planned than just moving his wife down the Florida coast.

———

On April 1, 1973, two men searching for aluminum cans to recycle on Hutchinson Island stumbled upon the scene of an execution. They found the decomposed remains of two young girls. The bodies had been buried in shallow graves, but animals had dug them up.

Using dental records, investigators identified the two female bodies as seventeen-year-old Susan Place and sixteen-year-old Georgia Jessup. Although the majority of their flesh was gone, at one time their arms and legs had been tied with rags. Both had nooses around their necks and the tree branches above showed signs of rope friction. They had been hanged.

Susan Place's body was missing a hand and forearm. Her left shoulder joint had been severed and her backbone had been cut through from the rear, all with a sharp instrument. Georgia Jessup's legs had been cut off just above the knee and her head had been severed. Her skull was never found. Her spine had been cut or separated by a knife of some sort.

The bodies had been found only a few miles from where Nancy and Sue had been assaulted. It was evident that the girls had been hung in the same manner that Schaefer had attempted to hang Nancy and Sue. Investigators instantly suspected Schaefer for the murders, but when the bodies were found, he was already in the county jail. He had been there for four months of his six-month sentence. Investigators needed to know if the girls had been dead for more than four months. Medical examiners, however, were unable to determine precisely when the girls had been killed. The bodies were too badly decomposed.

————

Detectives spoke to the families of both Georgia Jessup and Susan Place at their homes in Fort Lauderdale. Susan's mother told detectives she had last seen the girls six months earlier on September 27 with a man in his twenties named Jerry Shepard. Not trusting the young man, Mrs. Place had taken down the license plate number of the young man's blue-green Datsun. When police checked the registration of the car, it belonged to Gerard Schaefer.

Mrs. Place also found a letter in Susan's bedroom that had been marked "Return to Sender." The letter was addressed to Jerry Shepard, but it was the prior home of Gerard Schaefer.

When the news of the murders was announced by the media, Schaefer contacted his wife from prison. Just before he went away to serve his jail sentence, he had given Teresa Schaefer a brown suede purse. Schaefer gave her no reason why, but told her she absolutely must get rid of the purse.

Prosecutors had plenty of circumstantial evidence that
Schaefer had murdered Susan Place and Georgia Jessup, but
they needed physical evidence. Knowing that and knowing
that her husband desperately wanted her to get rid of it,
Teresa handed over the purse to police. Georgia Jessup's
mother identified the purse as one that she had given to her
daughter for her birthday.

Georgia Jessup / Nancy Trotter / Susan Place

Investigators believed that Georgia and Susan were killed
sometime between September 27, 1972, when he picked up
the girls, and January 1973, when Schaefer went to jail. He
had been out on bail and had his jail sentence delayed, giving
him the perfect window of opportunity.

That April, investigators searched the home of Schaefer's
mother, where he had stored all of his belongings. They
found orange crates and a steamer trunk packed full of
potential evidence of additional murders.

Stashed at his mother's house, investigators found several pieces of jewelry, a driver's license, a passport, two gold teeth, an address book, a purse, clothing, a diary, and a book of poetry. Many of the items had belonged to several other girls that had gone missing in the area.

Also in the steamer trunk, police found several newspaper clippings about missing girls. But even more disturbing were hundreds of pages of Schaefer's own handwritten stories, each describing horrific rapes, tortures, necrophilia, cannibalism, and murders of women in which he referred to the women as "whores" and "sluts." Although Schaefer claimed the stories were nothing more than pulp fiction, police believed they were confessions. Some of the stories accurately described the traumatic abduction and escape of Nancy Trotter and Paula Sue Wells.

On September 27, 1973, Gerard John Schaefer went on trial for the two murders and was quickly found guilty. Both Nancy Trotter and Paula Sue Wells testified against him and provided the jury with a reenactment of the abduction and assault. He was sentenced to serve two consecutive life terms.

––––––

Although Schaefer would spend the rest of his life behind bars, investigators knew he was responsible for far more than just the two murders. Over the years, the items found in Schaefer's mother's house were linked to several other missing girls.

The passport, driver's license, diary, and a book of poetry belonged to Collette Goodenough and Barbara Wilcox, two nineteen-year-old hitchhikers that had gone missing in 1971. Their decapitated remains were found in 1977 in Martin county.

A shamrock pin and the two gold-filled teeth were linked to twenty-two-year-old Carmen Hallock—missing since 1969. A gold locket with the name "Leigh" belonged to Schaefer's former neighbor, Leigh Hainline Bonadies, who he had claimed taunted him from her bedroom window. Two additional pieces of her jewelry were in his possession, as well as a newspaper clipping of her disappearance. Her skull was discovered in the area in 1978, containing multiple bullet holes.

Other items belonged to fourteen-year-old Mary Briscolina and thirteen-year-old Elsie Farmer whose headless bodies were found in 1973.

The mementos in Schaefer's possession were linked to thirty-eight other girls. All girls were either missing or murdered with the cases dating back to 1966. Police believed all the items were trophies that Schaefer had taken from his victims. Some in law enforcement believed there could have been many more victims.

———

Two weeks after his conviction, Schaefer's wife Teresa divorced him and, two days later, married the public defender that represented him at trial. Despite claiming that his attorney and his wife had conspired against him, Schaefer continued to use the same attorney to file twenty appeals. All of these were denied.

Throughout his years in prison, Schaefer worked as a "jailhouse lawyer" for himself and other inmates. Much of the information he attained from other inmates, however, was later used against them at trial. He had been working with prosecutors. He also became known for filing frivolous libel lawsuits against reporters and writers for everything from inaccurately stating his kill count to calling him "overweight."

Schaefer continued writing his horrific stories in prison. After twenty years of incarceration, Schaefer teamed up with a former girlfriend from his childhood, Sondra London, to have his stories published. In one story entitled "Murder Demons", he recounted how he had murdered Mary Briscolina and Elsie Farmer. He was careful, however, to word the stories in a way as to not implicate himself, claiming the stories were entirely fiction. Despite the accurate detail of the stories, detectives were unable to use any information to convict him of additional murders.

In 1991 Schaefer wrote a personal letter to his co-author, Sondra London:

> "What crimes am I supposed to confess? Farmer? Briscolina? What do you think 'Murder Demons' is? You want confessions but don't recognize them when I anoint you with them and we've just gotten started."

There was much speculation over what Schaefer's actual kill count was. Although experts believe the number is between 32 and 40, Schaefer himself wrote that his actual kill count was somewhere between 80 and 110.

> "I've always harped on District Attorney Robert Stone's list of 34. In 1973, I sat down and drew up a list of my own. I'm not claiming a huge number. I would say it runs between 80

and 110. But over eight years and three continents. One whore drowned in her own vomit while watching me disembowel her girlfriend. I'm not sure that counts as a valid kill. Did the pregnant ones count as two kills? It can get confusing."

———

Sondra London handed the personal letters over to police. Using the letters, police were able to re-open three cases in hopes of finding additional clues to convict him of more than just the two murders. Detectives arranged to speak with Schaefer in December 1995, but there would be no need. Just days before the scheduled interview, Schaefer was murdered in his jail cell.

Gerard John Schaefer had been attacked by a fellow inmate named Vincent Rivera. His mouth had been slit from ear to ear and he had been stabbed eighteen times in each eye with a prison shank. Motive for the killing was a mystery. Many speculated Rivera had killed Schaefer for snitching on other inmates, while some believed it had something to do with information he had about Ottis Toole's confession of murdering Adam Walsh. Still others believed Schaefer was killed simply over an argument about a cup of coffee.

Gerard Schaefer / Vincent Rivera / Jewelry found in Schaefer's possession.

Regardless of why he was killed, all hopes of closure had been vanquished for dozens of families of young women across the southeast.

13

BONUS CHAPTER: THE JACKSONVILLE MONSTER

This chapter is a **free bonus chapter** from True Crime Case Histories: Volume 6

On a Sunday morning in 1992, thirteen-year-old Kerri Anne Buck walked toward her friend's house through her suburban neighborhood in Jacksonville, Florida, when she heard the low rumble of a vehicle pulling up behind her. Kerri Anne turned around to see a white van with tinted windows slowing down beside her.

The passenger side window of the van rolled down and the driver, a man in his thirties, called out, "Do you know Susie?" Kerri Anne replied "No" and continued walking. Slowly rolling beside her as she walked, the man then said, "Do you go to Southside Middle School?" His voice sounded angry to the young girl. She replied, "No," which was a lie.

The man was a stranger. Kerri Anne knew better than to talk to strangers. The man then stopped the van and commanded her to,

"Get the fuck in the van!"

Kerri Anne ran down the street as fast as she could. When she reached her friend's house and pounded on the door, there was no answer. She knew the neighborhood well and continued running around the corner to a large park as the man ran after her. In the park, Kerri Anne found a playground which had a children's slide shaped into a tube. She climbed the ladder, slid halfway down the tube, stopped, and wedged herself against the walls of the slide.

Kerri Anne could hear the man entering the area around the playground as she pushed harder and harder against the walls, trying not to slip out the bottom of the tube. She heard him grunt

"I know you're in there, you little bitch. I'm going to find you."

She waited for what seemed like an eternity and eventually got up the courage to peek out. He was gone. For the time being, Kerri Anne was safe. She ran back home as fast as she could.

Kerri Anne and her parents were on edge for several days afterward and Kerri was frightened to step foot outside their home. A few weeks after the incident, Kerri Anne's mother saw a strange white van parked outside their house. Mrs. Buck called her daughter to the window and Kerri Anne confirmed that it was the van of the man that tried to abduct her. Kerri's mother took down the license plate and called the police.

The owner of the van was thirty-six-year-old Donald Smith – and it wasn't his first brush with the law. Smith had been in and out of prison for sex crimes since the 1970s. As a registered sex offender, Smith was quickly arrested and sentenced to six years in prison for the attempted kidnapping of Kerri Anne Buck.

Prison was no deterrent for Smith. When he was released in the late nineties, he continued to prey on children. His obsession was insatiable. He was in and out of prison for the next fifteen years for crimes ranging from selling obscene material, voyeurism, and public masturbation, to felony child abuse.

In 2009 Smith was charged with impersonating a public employee and aggravated child abuse by willful torture. He had posed as a child welfare case worker, got a ten-year-old girl on the phone, asked her sexually explicit questions, and threatened to harm her.

After serving less than fifteen months in Jackson County Jail for the crime, the repeat sexual offender was released once again on May 31, 2013.

———

Rayne Perrywinkle had fallen on hard times – but then again, times were always hard for Rayne. Although she had given up her first-born daughter twenty years prior to relatives in Australia, she was doing her best to raise her three youngest daughters by herself in Jacksonville.

Eight-year-old Cherish Perrywinkle was the oldest of the girls living with Rayne. Rayne had had a very brief relationship with Cherish's father, Billy Jarreau. To put it bluntly, it was a one-night-stand. In 2003 she had been a stripper, Billy a recently divorced Navy officer, when they met at a Jacksonville strip club. After several nights of lap dances, Billy convinced her to go home with him. Nine months later, Cherish was born.

Initially Billy contested his paternity. He was willing to provide support for the girl, but needed proof that he was the father. Eventually a court-ordered paternity test proved he was indeed Cherish's father, so he accepted her with open arms and financial support.

Despite the financial support, Rayne continued to struggle to get her life on track. She had two more girls with another man but never married, while Billy believed Cherish would be better off living with him in California. He tried several times to get custody of the girl, but each time failed. Instead, Rayne agreed to let Cherish spend summers with her father in California.

———

On June 21, 2013, Rayne was reluctantly getting ready to send Cherish to California for the summer. The flight was scheduled for the next day and Rayne took her three girls to the Dollar General store to get Cherish some clothes for the trip. They shopped in the store for over an hour, unaware that sixty-one-year-old Donald Smith was watching them from afar.

Cherish Perrywinkle

Rayne and Cherish found a little black and white dress with hearts that they liked, but when Rayne asked the cashier the price of the dress, she realized she didn't have enough money to buy it and still pay for a taxi to the airport the next day.

Donald Smith had come into the store just minutes before and asked the cashier if they had any adult magazines. When Smith overheard Rayne explain to the cashier that she couldn't afford the dress, he took notice. He could tell that Rayne was frustrated and struggling to provide for her young girls.

When Rayne and the girls left the store, Smith approached Rayne outside of the store and said, "If you really want that dress, I'll get it for you. You look like you really have your hands full. I have a couple of little ones myself."

At first glance, he seemed harmless enough. Just an older gentleman – a good Samaritan. Rayne had no way of knowing he was a deranged predator that had been released from prison only three weeks earlier.

Smith introduced himself as Don and explained to her that he was waiting for his wife to arrive. He claimed his wife had a Walmart gift card for $150 that he was willing to give to her to help buy Cherish some clothes. Rayne was apprehensive about talking to a complete stranger, but he spoke at length about his own young children and wife—none of which existed. He told her he worked for the charity Habitat for Humanity—another lie.

When Rayne informed him that she needed to get home and get Cherish ready for her flight, he told her to be patient and encouraged her to wait. His wife would show up any minute and she would be driving a gold car. He then reached into his pocket, opened his phone, and pretended to talk to someone on the other end. After the call he said, "That was my wife. She's just going to meet us at Walmart."

Walmart was ten minutes away and Rayne didn't own a car. She had no way to get there other than by taxi, but of course, Smith offered to take them in his van. Still feeling uneasy, she declined at first, but he insisted he was no threat. "Do you want to see my driver's license or something?" He did his best to make her feel foolish for being paranoid, so eventually she accepted the ride.

When they arrived at Walmart around 9:00 p.m., Rayne and the girls entered the store while Smith faked another phone call. He then told Rayne that his wife had called and the two of them would like to take them out for dinner after shopping, but Rayne had no intention of going out to dinner with them. Her only concern was getting the gift card for her kids and going home.

Cherish tried on clothes for over an hour and a half while Rayne put the girls' items into her push cart. The only item Smith put in the cart was some rope that he picked up in the hardware department. As he watched the girls shopping, Rayne was shocked when Cherish brought a pair of women's high heel shoes to her and asked if she could try them on.

She immediately told her, "No, those aren't kids' shoes! Where did you get those?" Cherish replied, "Don wanted me to try them on." Rayne told him, "Those are women's high heels! I wouldn't even wear heels that high!"

After shopping for almost two hours, Smith's wife still hadn't arrived. Each time Rayne asked where she was, he just replied that she was "on her way." At 10:30 p.m., Walmart announced that the store would be closing in thirty minutes. The girls were getting tired and hadn't had any dinner yet. Smith held his hand up next to his face imitating a sock-puppet and said to the girls, "I'm going to McDonald's. What do you want to eat?" All the girls screamed "cheeseburgers!"

Smith started walking toward the McDonald's restaurant located within the Walmart store near the front entrance and Cherish followed him. Rayne was initially concerned, but Smith had spent the entire night making Rayne feel over-protective. She knew there were security cameras all over the store and believed there was no chance he could disappear with her daughter. Ignoring her better judgement, Rayne let her daughter follow the man she had met only hours ago.

Donald Smith (mugshot & Walmart security footage) and Rayne Perrywinkle

Knowing the store was closing soon, Rayne and her two girls finished up their shopping and pushed their cart toward the front of the store. When they got to the McDonald's, Cherish and Donald Smith were nowhere to be found. Rayne pushed her cart with a quickened pace back and forth along the front of the store, looking down each aisle for her daughter. As she passed each empty aisle, she felt her heart beating harder and harder. With each step, she became more and more panicked.

When Walmart announced they were closing for the night and she couldn't find her daughter, terror overwhelmed her. Rayne was frantic and asked for help from Walmart employees, "Call 911, my daughter's been taken!" Rayne didn't have a working phone of her own and asked them to call, but the Walmart employees didn't take her seriously. The store was massive and the employees just assumed the young girl was lost.

Rayne continued to panic. She looked through the store and in the parking lot, but there was no sign of her daughter or Smith's white van. After 11:00 p.m., the store had closed and Rayne hadn't seen her daughter for a full thirty minutes before a Walmart employee finally let her borrow a cell phone.

During the heart-wrenching 911 call, Rayne explained the events of the day as police rushed to the scene:

> "... I had a bad feeling, I thought, well, I feel like pinching myself cause this is too good to be true, so I got to the checkout and he's not here and I'm hoping he's not raping her right now, cause I've had that done to me. I don't understand why he would leave right now unless he was gonna rape her and kill her - that's the only reason. And I'm wasting my time standing here!"

Rayne was so distressed she couldn't even remember what her daughter had been wearing that day. Throughout the night Rayne described the van and Smith's appearance to police. Using the description and checking the local sex offender registration, police quickly knew they were looking for Donald Smith. By 4:00 a.m., police had issued an Amber alert. By morning, the entire area of Jacksonville was looking for Cherish, Smith, and Smith's white van.

Just after 7:00 a.m., police received a call from a woman in north Jacksonville. She had seen a white van parked in an odd spot. It was discreetly parked in some bushes behind a church. It seemed suspicious to the woman because it was wedged deeply into the bushes. The woman suspected that someone in the van had dumped something in the bushes, but when police arrived and did the initial search of the area, they found nothing.

Smith lived with his mother. The police had already been to her house looking for him, but she claimed she had no idea where he was. After they left the house, police received a call from a man that rented a room at the Smith home. He told police that the prior afternoon, he had helped Smith remove the middle row of seats from his van. He also said that Smith had told him that if he ever had to run from the police, he would hide in the woods near a homeless camp in the area. Smith had told the man that he knew someone that had lived at the camp for twenty-eight years without police ever bothering him.

Every division of law enforcement in the area was on the lookout for Smith's 1998 white Dodge van. It didn't take long to find him. Before noon the morning after the abduction, Smith was pulled over and arrested... but there was no trace of Cherish. When the arresting officer noticed his pants were soaking wet, he yelled to the other officers, "Oh my God, she's in the water!"

Police rushed back to the Highlands Baptist Church. The earlier caller's suspicions were correct. The same officer that arrested Smith found the body of eight-year-old Cherish Perrywinkle wedged under a tree in a marshy wetland behind the church. Her body had been weighed down with chunks of asphalt and hidden with grass and branches. She was still wearing the bright orange dress with a fruit pattern on it, but naked beneath it. Her underwear and purple flip-flops were never found.

The sixty-seven pound girl had been gagged, raped, and sodomized for hours before she was strangled to death with a piece of clothing. The massive force of the trauma caused her gums, nostrils, and eyes to bleed. A forensic pathologist that examined Cherish's body would later tell the court, "She had so much trauma, her anatomy was totally distorted by the trauma she suffered."

———

The trial of Donald Smith didn't begin until February 2018, almost five years later. Smith faced the death penalty if found guilty. The trial was incredibly emotional as Rayne Perrywinkle recounted the horrifying evening. The jury was shown photos of the young girl that made them gasp out loud and cover their eyes. Some cried out loud. Even Smith turned his back and couldn't look at the autopsy photos of Cherish.

The Walmart and Dollar General security camera footage evidence against him left very little doubt of his guilt. When asked if the defense wanted to cross-examine Rayne, Smith said,

> "I don't want her to go through anything she doesn't have to go through. I'm done."

The jurors took only fifteen minutes to convict Donald Smith of kidnapping, rape, and murder. The week following his conviction, the jurors were asked if he should spend life in prison or be executed. New constitutional guidelines required a unanimous decision; every juror chose the death penalty.

At sentencing, Judge Mallory Cooper's voice cracked with emotion when she told Smith,

> "Donald Smith, you have not only forfeited your right to live among us, you have forfeited your right to live at all. May God have mercy on your soul."

───────

After suffering the loss of her daughter, Rayne Perrywinkle's troubles were not over. The public condemned her, blaming her for leaving her daughter alone with Smith. Some went so far as to speculate that she was somehow involved in human trafficking. It didn't help matters when it came out during a deposition that Rayne claimed she was a clairvoyant and had a vision that her daughter would be dead by the time she was eight years old.

After the death of Cherish, Rayne was unable to shake the extreme grief of the traumatic event topped off with the blame from the public. She couldn't keep a job and was often turned down because everyone knew her name.

The state of Florida gave her twelve months to show that she could provide for her two remaining daughters, but it wasn't enough. Nine-year-old Destiny and seven-year-old Nevaeh were inevitably adopted by Rayne's sister and now live with their older sister, Lindsay, in Australia.

———

This chapter is a free bonus chapter from True Crime Case Histories: Volume 6

Online Appendix

Visit my website for additional photos and videos pertaining to the cases in this book:

http://TrueCrimeCaseHistories.com/vol7/

Also by Jason Neal

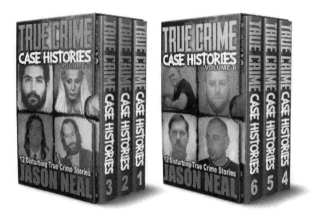

Looking for more?? I am constantly adding new volumes of True Crime Case Histories and all books are also available in paperback, hardcover and audiobooks.

Check out the complete series on Amazon:

Amazon US / Amazon UK

**FREE Bonus Book
For My Readers**

<u>Click to get
your free copy!</u>

As my way of saying "Thank you" for downloading, I'm giving away a FREE true crime book I think you'll enjoy.

http://truecrimecasehistories.com

Just click the link above to let me know where to send your free gift!

Choose Your Free True Crime Audiobook

Switch between listening to an audiobook and reading on your Kindle. **Plus choose your first audiobook for FREE!** Audible US / Audible UK

THANK YOU!

Thank you for reading my seventh Volume of True Crime Case Histories. I truly hope you enjoyed it. If you did, I would be sincerely grateful if you would take a few minutes to write a review for me on Amazon using the link below.

http://truecrime.page/book7

I'd also like to encourage you to sign-up for my email list for updates, discounts and freebies on future books! I promise I'll make it worth your while with future freebies.

http://truecrimecasehistories.com

And please take a moment and follow me on Amazon

http://truecrime.page/amazonUS

http://truecrime.page/amazonUK

One last thing. I would love to hear your feedback and personal thoughts on the book. I have found that many people that aren't regular readers of true crime can't handle the horrible details of stories like these. Do you think the level of detail is ok, or would you rather see it toned down a bit? Or if you'd like to contact me for any other reason free to email me at:

jasonnealbooks@gmail.com

Thanks so much,

Jason Neal

ABOUT THE AUTHOR

Jason Neal is a Best-Selling American True Crime Author living in Hawaii with his Turkish-British wife. Jason started his writing career in the late eighties as a music industry publisher and wrote his first true crime collection in 2019.

As a boy growing up in the eighties just south of Seattle, Jason became interested in true crime stories after hearing the news of the Green River Killer so close to his home. Over the subsequent years he would read everything he could get his hands on about true crime and serial killers.

As he approached 50, Jason began to assemble stories of the crimes that have fascinated him most throughout his life. He's especially obsessed by cases solved by sheer luck, amazing police work, and groundbreaking technology like early DNA cases and more recently reverse genealogy.

Printed in Great Britain
by Amazon

78431135R00120